OXFORD

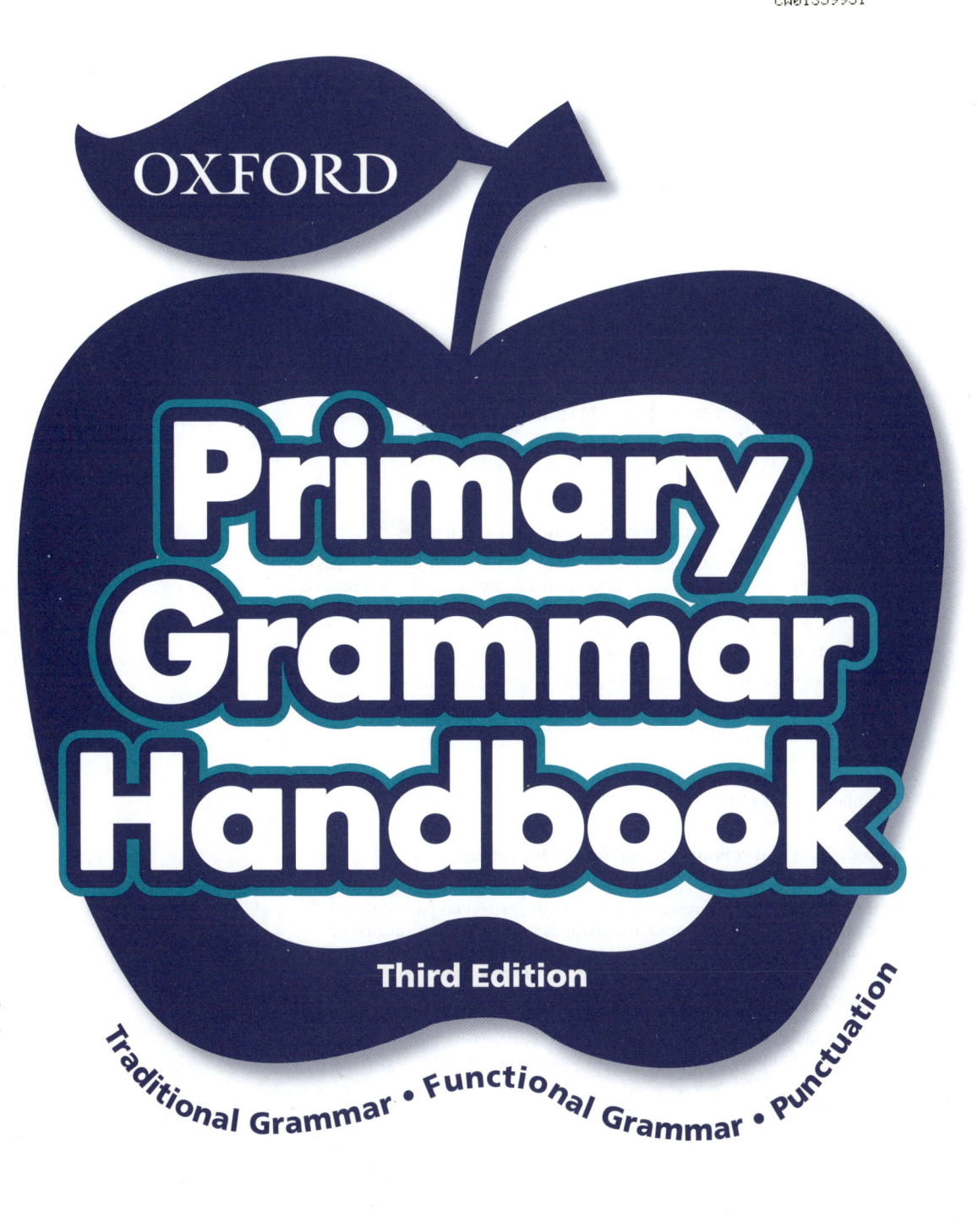

Primary Grammar Handbook

Third Edition

Traditional Grammar • Functional Grammar • Punctuation

Gordon Winch
Gregory Blaxell

OXFORD
UNIVERSITY PRESS

253 Normanby Road, South Melbourne, Victoria 3205, Australia

Oxford University Press is a department of the University of Oxford.
It furthers the University's objective of excellence in research, scholarship,
and education by publishing worldwide in

Oxford New York

Auckland Cape Town Dar es Salaam Hong Kong Karachi
Kuala Lumpur Madrid Melbourne Mexico City Nairobi
New Delhi Shanghai Taipei Toronto

With offices in

Argentina Austria Brazil Chile Czech Republic France Greece
Guatemala Hungary Italy Japan Poland Portugal Singapore
South Korea Switzerland Thailand Turkey Ukraine Vietnam

OXFORD is a trademark of Oxford University Press
in the UK and in certain other countries

Copyright © Gordon Winch and Gregory Blaxell 2007

First edition published 1994 by Horwitz Martin Education
Revised edition published 1999
Reprinted 2005 by Oxford University Press
Third edition published 2007
Reprinted 2008

Reproduction and communication for educational purposes

The Australian *Copyright Act 1968* (the Act) allows a maximum of one chapter
or 10% of the pages of this work, whichever is the greater, to be reproduced
and/or communicated by any educational institution for its educational purposes
provided that the educational institution (or the body that administers it) has
given a remuneration notice to Copyright Agency Limited (CAL) under the Act.

For details of the CAL licence for educational institutions contact:

Copyright Agency Limited
Level 15, 233 Castlereagh Street
Sydney NSW 2000
Telephone: (02) 9394 7600
Facsimile: (02) 9394 7601
E-mail: info@copyright.com.au

Reproduction and communication for other purposes

Except as permitted under the Act (for example, any fair dealing
for the purposes of study, research, criticism or review) no part of this
book may be reproduced, stored in a retrieval system, communicated or
transmitted in any form or by any means without prior written permission.
All enquiries should be made to the publisher at the address above.

National Library of Australia Cataloguing-in-Publication data:

Winch, Gordon, 1930–.
The primary grammar handbook : traditional and functional
grammar, punctuation and usage.

3rd ed.
Includes index.
For primary school students.
ISBN 9780195560282.

1. English language—Grammar—Juvenile literature.
I. Blaxell, Gregory. II. Title.

Typeset in India by diacriTech Chennai
Illustrated by Annie White
Printed in China by Golden Cup Printing Co. Ltd

Contents

To the student — v

To the teacher — v

Introduction — vi

Word level: the parts of speech
Nouns — 1
Pronouns — 6
Adjectives — 15
Verbs — 19
Adverbs — 29
Prepositions — 32
Conjunctions — 34
Articles — 36
Interjections — 37
Parsing — 37

Phrase level
Phrases — 39

Clause level
Clauses — 43

Sentence level
Sentences — 47
Analysis of sentences — 51

Text level
Traditional and functional grammar — 52

Functional grammar
Introduction — 57
Genres or text types — 57
   Literary texts — 58
      Narrative — 58
      Literary recount — 60
      Literary description — 61
      Literary review — 64
      Poetry — 66
   Factual texts — 67
      Factual description — 67
      Information report — 68

Procedure	69
Factual recount	70
Explanation	72
Exposition	73
Discussion	75
Register/social context	77
Differences in texts	79
Clause structures to represent experience	81
Language structure of personal interaction	81
Language structures for constructing texts	82
Sentences in functional grammar	83
More about verbs	84
More about nouns	84
Traditional/functional terms	85
Some additional terms	87

Punctuation

Capital letters	90
Full stops	90
Question marks	92
Exclamation marks	92
Commas	92
Quotation, direct speech marks	94
Apostrophes	95
Semicolons	96
Colons	97
Brackets	97
Dashes	97
Hyphens	98
Ellipses	98

Correct usage

Confused words	99
Homonyms	117
Making sense	142
Improving your writing	143
Origins of words and figurative language	146
Index	148

To the student

This book is about grammar, which tells you how language works. You will be able to use it to learn the meanings of terms like **conjunction**, **preposition** or **clause**, how words are used correctly, how different types of writing are put together, and how they are used for different purposes.

To the teacher

Children come to school with a remarkably sophisticated grammar of English. They apply this grammar automatically, and with growing accuracy, in their speech. It is, however, an implicit knowledge because they cannot describe it or even understand the terminology needed to describe it. This grammar has been acquired by contact with other speakers of the language and by the use of an inherent linguistic ability, unique to humans.

At school, students will learn grammatical terminology and will be able to develop an **explicit** knowledge of the grammar of their language. This will enable them to discuss their speech, reading and writing and will provide an essential tool for the successful development of literacy skills.

Introduction

The Primary Grammar Handbook is a reference book to English grammar, punctuation and usage. It contains both traditional and functional grammars, a section that shows how many of the terms used in traditional and functional grammar relate to one another, and a reference to origins of words and the use of figurative language in English.

This handbook has been written to provide school children with a text that gives ready access to basic grammatical concepts and correct spoken and written English found in a variety of contexts.

Traditional and functional grammar

Traditional grammar has proved to be very useful for practical purposes. It provides students with a language to describe language, a **metalanguage** as linguists call it. It is essential to the study of foreign languages. It provides a basis for correct judgment on the different forms of usage. It also establishes a conceptual base and terminology for the learning of other grammars, such as functional grammar.

Functional grammar, based on systemic linguistics, emphasises the way spoken and written language operates in different situations. In particular, it is very useful in showing how texts work beyond the level of the sentence, how different texts are structured and how language varies to suit the purpose of the users. Its principles have found their way into an increasing number of English syllabuses and its inclusion in this text, together with the section that shows the comparison with traditional grammar, will be very useful for teachers and students.

Acknowledgment

The extract from *The Nargun and the Stars* on pages 62–4 is reproduced by arrangement with the licensor, Patricia Wrightson c/o Curtis Brown (Aust.) Pty Ltd.

WORD LEVEL: THE PARTS OF SPEECH

Nouns

What is a noun? *(See also Noun phrases p. 41, Noun group/phrase p. 83 and Participants pp. 80, 81, 84, 86)*

A **noun** is the name of a person, place or thing.

There are four main kinds of nouns: *common nouns*, *proper nouns*, *collective nouns* and *abstract nouns*.

Girl is a noun.

John is a noun.

Crowd is a noun.

Happiness is a noun, even though you can't see or touch it.

Common nouns

A **common noun** is the special name of any ordinary thing you can see and touch.

These are common nouns:

apple	mountain	beach
boy	bell	cow
hat	garden	dog

The **apple** is bad.
Common noun

Proper nouns

A **proper noun** is the special name of a person, place or thing. Proper nouns start with capital letters.

These are proper nouns:

Christmas	Monday	Australia
Emily	France	Easter
Canberra	Kim	Captain Smith

Emily is my friend.
Proper noun

Collective nouns

A collective noun is the name given to a group of persons or things.

These are collective nouns:

class	team	band
herd	litter	pack
convoy	swarm	bunch

A swarm of bees
Collective noun

Abstract nouns

An abstract noun is the name of something that could exist in your mind, although you cannot see or touch it.

These are abstract nouns:

hope	sadness	kindness
love	joy	beauty
despair	greed	anger

Love is everywhere.
Abstract noun

🍎 Other noun types

Terms of address nouns

Terms of address nouns are nouns we use when we are talking or writing to someone.

These are terms of address nouns:

Mrs Jones   Johnno   Your Highness

They are special types of proper nouns.

Good morning, Mrs Jones.
Terms of address noun

Technical nouns

Technical nouns refer to a particular field of study.

These are technical nouns:

fraction	narrative
oxygen	mammal

A bear is a mammal.
Technical noun

Count and mass nouns

A count or countable noun is a noun that can be counted, such as apple, leg or dog.

A mass or non-countable noun refers to a noun that cannot be counted, such as information, traffic or advice. You do not refer to informations, traffics or advices.

We saw two lions at the zoo.
Count noun

What heavy traffic!
Mass or non-count noun

Concrete nouns

A concrete noun refers to things you can see or touch, like tree, hat or nose. It is the opposite of an abstract noun, which is something you cannot touch, such as joy or sadness.

Two tall trees
Concrete noun

More about nouns

Nouns and pronouns have **person**. Person refers to who is speaking, who is spoken to or who is spoken about. All nouns are in the **third person**; they are always spoken about. *(See also More about pronouns, which can be first, second or third person, pp. 10–11)*

The sun is shining.
Third person

Number

A noun has number. It can be **singular** or **plural**. Singular means one; plural means more than one.

SINGULAR	PLURAL
leg	legs

Many singular nouns add **s** to make the plural.

boy	boys
girl	girls
toy	toys

leg
singular

Others add **es**.

| beach | beaches |
| fox | foxes |

legs
plural

If a noun ends in **y** and has a consonant before the **y**, the plural drops the **y** and adds **ies**.

baby   babies
lady   ladies

baby
singular

babies
plural

Nouns ending in **f** or **fe** make the plural in two ways.

- They add **s**.

chief   chiefs

- They change the **f** to **v** and add **es**.

knife   knives
loaf   loaves

Nouns ending in **o** make the plural in two ways.

- They add **s**.

piano   pianos
merino   merinos

merino
singular

merinos
plural

- They add **es**.

potato   potatoes
tomato   tomatoes

Compound nouns are made from two or more words.

They make the plural in two ways.

- They add **s**.

spoonful   spoonfuls

- They add **s** to the first part of the compound.

brother-in-law   brothers-in-law

Some singular nouns that come from foreign words change their endings altogether.

crisis   crises
plateau   plateaux

Some singular nouns change their vowels to form the plural.

man   men

Sometimes they change their consonants as well.

mouse   mice

mouse
singular

Some singular nouns do not need to change the plural.

deer   deer

mice
plural

Always use your dictionary to check plurals that might have different spellings.

Gender

Nouns can be male or female. If a noun is neither male nor female, it is neuter. Male, female and neuter are called gender.

Some nouns like *child* or *animal* can be both masculine and feminine. These nouns are said to be *common* gender.

MASCULINE	FEMININE	NEUTER	COMMON
boy	girl	rock	child

Case

Nouns and pronouns have case.

There are three main cases: *nominative*, also called *subjective* (subject of a verb); *objective* (object of a verb or preposition); and *possessive* (showing ownership).

Ali saw Jenny's book.

NOMINATIVE CASE	OBJECTIVE CASE	POSSESSIVE CASE
Ali	book	Jenny's

To find the case of a word you need to do these things:

Nominative — Ask *who* or *what* in front of the verb.

Who saw? Answer: **Ali** (nominative case)

Objective — Ask *who* or *what* after the verb.

Saw what? Answer: **book** (objective case)

Possessive — Ask *whose*.

Whose book? Answer: **Jenny's** (possessive case)

Gerunds (verbal nouns)

Sometimes verbs ending in -ing are used as nouns. They are called gerunds or verbal nouns.

Here are some examples:

Running is good exercise.

I like eating.

I am good at fishing.

Running in the first sentence is a gerund in the nominative case, subject of the verb *is*.

Eating in the second sentence is a gerund in the objective case, object of the verb *like*.

Fishing in the third sentence is a gerund in the objective case, object of the preposition *at*.

! Important

Don't confuse gerunds with participles that do the job of adjectives.

> I went on a *walking* tour.

Walking is an adjective in the sentence. *(See Participles p. 21)*

Pronouns

? What is a pronoun? *(See also Participants pp. 80, 81, 84, 86)*

A **pronoun** is a word that is used in place of a noun.

> Maria is a girl. *She* will be ten on Sunday.

The word **Maria** is a noun. The word **she** is used in its place. **She** is a pronoun. There are different kinds of pronouns. In the following sentences, the pronouns are highlighted.

> *She* is ten on Sunday.
>
> The book is *mine*.
>
> I know the boy *who* was hurt.
>
> *That* is my dog.

> *What* is the time?
>
> He hit *himself* with a hammer.
>
> *Anyone* can do it.
>
> *Each* has a bicycle.

Personal pronouns

Personal pronouns are used in place of persons or things.

Like the nouns they represent, they may be the **subject** or **part of the subject** of the sentence.

> *She* is ten on Sunday.
>
> *She* and James are ten on Sunday.

They are said to be in the **nominative** case.

She and James are ten on Sunday. **Personal pronoun**

The personal pronouns in the nominative case are:

SINGULAR	I	you	he she it
PLURAL	we	you	they

Notice that *you* can be either singular or plural.

A personal pronoun may be the **object** or **indirect object** in a sentence.

> Kim saw *them*.
>
> Ali gave *me* the book.

This really means 'Ali gave the book to me'. Therefore *me* in the sentence 'Ali gave me the book' is called an *indirect object*.

A personal pronoun can be the object of a preposition.

> The teacher gave the pies to her.

Them, ***me*** and ***her*** are said to be in the ***objective case***.

The personal pronouns in the objective case are:

SINGULAR	me	you	him her it
PLURAL	us	you	them

Again, *you* can be singular or plural.

Possessive pronouns

Possessive pronouns show ownership.

> That book is mine.

That book is mine.
Possessive pronoun

The possessive pronouns are:

SINGULAR	mine	yours	his hers its
PLURAL	ours	yours	theirs

There are some words that are like pronouns but are only used with a noun. They are called possessive adjectives *(see p. 15)*.

Relative pronouns

Relative pronouns relate to a noun or personal pronoun. This noun or pronoun is called an antecedent.

The relative pronoun has to agree with the antecedent in person and number.

> David, who is only eight years old, is playing in a band.

Some relative pronouns are:

> who   whom   which   that

The relative pronouns *who* and *whom*

We use the relative pronouns who and whom when we refer to people.

> The boy who lives next door

The relative pronoun *who* agrees in person and number with its antecedent, *boy*; that is, it is the same person and number. *Who* is nominative case because it is the subject of the verb *lives*.

> She disliked the captain whom you chose.

The relative pronoun *whom* refers to *captain*, which is its antecedent. *Whom* agrees in person and number with its antecedent, *captain*; that is, it is the same person and number.

7

Whom is objective case because it is the object of the verb ***chose***.

The relative pronoun ***whom*** is also used when it is governed by a preposition.

>the mate with whom I go to the movies

The relative pronoun is ***whom*** because it is governed by the preposition ***with*** and is in the objective case.

> **who and whom in modern usage**
>
> Modern usage seems to be moving away from the objective form ***whom*** and replacing it with ***who***. You will find many examples of this.

The relative pronouns which and that

We use the relative pronouns which and that when we refer to animals, places or things.

>You can catch the train, which goes every ten minutes.
>
>**OR** You can catch the train that goes in ten minutes.

Which and ***that*** both refer to the word ***train***, which is the antecedent. Notice the difference in meaning between the two sentences. The first one refers to a train that goes every ten minutes; the second refers to a particular train that goes in ten minutes. (Hurry or you'll miss it!)

Interrogative pronouns

Interrogative pronouns, sometimes called question pronouns, are used to ask questions.

>What is the right answer?

The interrogative pronouns are:

>who   whom   whose   which   what

If these words are followed by a noun, they become ***interrogative adjectives*** or ***pronominal adjectives***.

>Which animal made that sound?

Demonstrative pronouns

Demonstrative pronouns stand for and refer to a noun.

>Those are stolen goods.

The demonstrative pronouns are:

>that   this   those   these

If these demonstrative pronouns are followed by a noun, they become ***demonstrative adjectives*** or ***pronominal adjectives***.

>This hat is mine.

Reflexive and emphatic pronouns

Reflexive and emphatic pronouns are made by adding -self (singular) and -selves (plural) to the personal pronoun.

However, each has a specific use.

Reflexive pronouns

He hurt **himself**.

Himself is a reflexive pronoun because it refers back to the ***he*** that is the subject of the sentence.

Emphatic pronouns

The Premier **himself** came to visit our school yesterday.

Himself is an emphatic pronoun because it emphasises the noun ***Premier***.

Indefinite pronouns

Indefinite pronouns do not refer to any particular antecedent or stand for any person, place or thing in particular.

No-one is to blame for this mess.

No-one is to blame for this mess.
Indefinite pronoun

Those indefinite pronouns ending with ***-one*** or ***-body*** refer to persons, while those ending in ***-thing*** refer to places or things.

Some indefinite pronouns are:

one	none	anyone	everyone
someone	no-one	somebody	anybody
nobody	anything	everything	

Indefinite pronouns are usually followed by a singular verb.

Distributive pronouns

Distributive pronouns point to separate things and therefore are always followed by a singular verb.

> **Each** has its wool clipped.

The distributive pronouns are:

> each   either   neither

If these words are followed by a noun, they become *distinctive adjectives* or *pronominal adjectives*.

> **Each** lamb has its wool clipped.

🍎 More about pronouns

Person

A pronoun has different forms depending on its person.
There are *three persons*. They are:

First person

This refers to the person who is speaking.

> **I** am an athlete.
> [personal pronoun, first person, singular number]

> **We** all run in the City to Surf.
> [personal pronoun, first person, plural number]

> It is **mine**.
> [possessive pronoun, first person, singular number]

**I am an athlete.
Personal pronoun, first person, singular number**

Second person

This refers to the person being spoken to.

> **You** will be late, Tom.
> [personal pronoun, second person, singular number]

> **You** will be late, children.
> [personal pronoun, second person, plural number]

> You have won the prize, Jo. It is **yours**.
> [possessive pronoun, second person, singular number]

You have won the prize, children. It is **yours**.
[possessive pronoun, second person, plural number]

Third person

This refers to the person being spoken about.

I wouldn't trust **him**.
[personal pronoun, third person, singular number]

Theirs are in the wash.
[possessive pronoun, third person, plural number]

I wouldn't trust him.
Personal pronoun, third person, singular number

Number

Pronouns have number. Some are singular and some are plural.

If the noun it refers to (the antecedent) is singular, the pronoun is singular. If the noun it refers to is plural, the pronoun is plural. In the examples that follow, the antecedents are included in brackets with an **S** for singular or a **P** for plural placed above each.

    S
It (bike) is made of metal.

The noun is singular, so the pronoun is singular.

    P
They (boys) always muck up when the teacher leaves the room.

The noun is plural, so the pronoun is plural.

Here are some more examples, showing how pronouns of all kinds have number:

  S   P
I (John Giles) would like **them** (footballers) to train more often.
[personal pronouns]

    S
That is **his** (John's).
[possessive pronoun]

     S
This (way) is how the job is done.
[demonstrative pronoun]

     P
These (answers) are all correct.
[demonstrative pronoun]

Gender

There are four *genders*. They are:

- **masculine**
  male
- **feminine**
  female
- **neuter**
  neither male nor female
- **common**
  either male or female

boy, he
masculine

woman, she
feminine

stone, it
neuter

doctor, he or she
common

As pronouns stand for nouns, they have gender. The pronoun has the same gender as its antecedent, the noun it stands for.

Some examples

The antecedent is in brackets following the pronoun and has an '**M**' for masculine gender, '**F**' for feminine gender, '**N**' for neuter gender and '**C**' for common gender written above the brackets.

  M   **F**
He (a boy) hit me (a girl).
[*He* is masculine and *me* is feminine.]

  F   **M**
Hers (a girl) is the same as mine (a boy).
[*Hers* is feminine and *mine* is masculine.]

  N
It (a building) will have to be demolished.
[*It* is neuter.]

M   N
I (Fred) have **nothing** (money) left to give.
[*I* is masculine and *nothing* is neuter.]

C   C
Anyone (man and woman) who knows him will join **us** (men and women) today.
[*Anyone* and *us* are common gender.]

Case

You give it to me!
Nominative Objective Objective

No! It's mine.
Possessive

Pronouns take their cases from the clauses they are in. They are either subjects (nominative) or objects (objective) or show possession (possessive).

		NOMINATIVE	OBJECTIVE	POSSESSIVE
	Singular	I	me	mine
		you	you	yours
PRONOUNS		he	him	his
		she	her	hers
		it	it	its
	Plural	we	us	ours
		you	you	yours
		they	them	theirs

He found the book but didn't give it back to her.

The pronouns are **he**, **it** and **her**.

He is a personal pronoun and is the subject of the verb ***found***.
As the subject, it is nominative case.

It is a personal pronoun (antecedent ***book***) and is the object of the verb ***give***.
As the object, it is objective case.

Her is a personal pronoun and is governed by the preposition ***to***.
Because of the preposition, it is objective case.

The very special verb *to be*

The verb *to be* is very special because it has its own rule, which is:

The verb to be takes the same case after it as before it.

This is because it links a subject to a complement, which is something that completes the meaning but is not an object. That is why the verb *to be*, in its many forms, is sometimes called a linking or relating verb.

The rule means that the nominative case form of the pronoun is used before and after the verb.

It is *she* who was lost.

It is the subject of the sentence and *she* is the complement. *Is* is a part of the verb *to be*. You might expect that *her* would be used instead of *she* because *her* is the normal objective form of the pronoun. But *she* is correct because it is the complement of the verb *is*.

> Modern usage is gradually changing this rule. The sentence in the following example is technically correct because of the verb *to be*. However, many people these days see this as being very old-fashioned, although it is still important in accurate writing.
>
> It is *they* who need to pull up their socks.

It is *they* who need to pull up their socks.
Nominative case after the verb *to be*

Adjectives

What is an adjective? *(See also Attribute and adjectival in functional grammar p. 85, Adjectival phrases p. 39 and Adjectival clauses p. 45)*

An **adjective** is a describing word. It describes (adds meaning to) a noun or pronoun.

| A tall boy | A small cat | She is happy. |

Tall is an adjective. It describes the noun *boy*.

Small is an adjective. It describes the noun *cat*.

Happy is an adjective. It describes a pronoun, *she*.

Adjectives are said to qualify nouns or pronouns. There are many types of adjectives. They all describe nouns or pronouns.

Descriptive or describing adjectives

These are the most common adjectives. **Big, small** and **happy** are descriptive adjectives. They tell us about the quality of a person or thing.

Descriptive adjectives can be divided into *factual adjectives* and *classifying adjectives*. Factual adjectives tell us about the qualities of a person or thing, as in *kind* person or *big* ship. Classifying adjectives place something into a group or type, as in *Siamese* cat or *Australian* history.

Possessive adjectives

These adjectives show possession. In the sentence **This is my book**, **my** is a possessive adjective.

These are the possessive adjectives:

	SINGULAR	PLURAL
1st person (speaking)	my	our
2nd person (spoken to)	your	your
3rd person (spoken about)	his her its	their

Possessive adjectives must be followed by a noun. Possessive adjectives are sometimes called *pronoun adjectives* or *pronominal adjectives*.

Numeral or numbering adjectives

Numeral adjectives describe the number or numerical order of things.

In *five* geese, *eleven* players and *ten* toes, *five, eleven* and *ten* are numeral adjectives describing the nouns that follow them. These numeral adjectives are called *cardinal* because they state the number of things.

When we say **the *fifth* boy to finish**, *fifth* is a numeral adjective, too, but it is also called an *ordinal* adjective because it states in which order the boy finished.

Numeral adjectives are sometimes called *quantity adjectives*.

The *fifth* boy to finish
Numeral adjective
Ordinal adjective

Demonstrative adjectives

These adjectives demonstrate or point out.

This, *that*, *these* and *those* are **demonstrative adjectives** in the following sentences:

This hat is mine.   *That* hat is yours.

These shoes are mine.   *Those* shoes are yours.

Demonstrative adjectives are sometimes called *pointing adjectives*.

Distributive adjectives

These adjectives point to separate things.

Each, *every*, *either* and *neither* are **distributive adjectives** in the following sentences:

Each dog was barking.   *Every* person must attend.

Either you or I will go.   *Neither* Bill nor Jane is here.

Interrogative adjectives

Interrogative adjectives ask questions.

Which, *what* and *whose* are interrogative adjectives in the following sentences:

Which animal made that sound?

What make of plane is that?

Whose friend is waiting?

Whose dog is that?
Interrogative adjective

Modal adjectives

Modal adjectives are describing words that show amounts of probability or certainty.

a possible event

a definite result

Indefinite adjectives

Indefinite adjectives refer to number but do not give the exact number.

Some, *few*, *many* and *most* are examples of indefinite adjectives in the following sentences:

Some people are very kind.

Few parents would come to the show.

Many children are swimming.

Most cars are shiny.

🍎 More about adjectives

Adjectives and degree

Most adjectives show what is called degree. Degree tells how much more or less.

There are three degrees:

POSITIVE	COMPARATIVE	SUPERLATIVE
big	bigger	biggest

Big is the first (positive), *bigger* is the second (comparative), *biggest* is the third (superlative).

Many adjectives take this form to show degree. Here are some others:

POSITIVE	COMPARATIVE	SUPERLATIVE
strong	stronger	strongest
soft	softer	softest
green	greener	greenest

Other adjectives seem clumsy if you add *-er* or *-est*. They form their comparative and superlative forms with the adverbs *more* or *most*, like these:

POSITIVE	COMPARATIVE	SUPERLATIVE
beautiful	more beautiful	most beautiful
delicate	more delicate	most delicate
reliable	more reliable	most reliable

Other adjectives have irregular forms:

POSITIVE	COMPARATIVE	SUPERLATIVE
good	better	best
many	more	most
little	less	least
bad	worse	worst

Positive only

Some adjectives do not have a comparative or superlative degree. They are sometimes called **absolute words**. *(See Making sense p. 142)*

Empty is one. If a thing is empty, it cannot be more empty.

Full is another, for the same reason. A thing cannot be more full.

Some adjectives like these are **dead**, **correct**, **straight** and **perfect**.

Fewer and less

Fewer refers to numbers of things; **less** refers to quantities.

Fewer people crossed the bridge.

Less butter is needed in the cake.

Fewer is always followed by a plural noun as in:

Fewer apples were on the tree.

Less is followed by a singular noun as in:

Less water was on the road.

Participles (verbal adjectives)

In the phrase **a walking tour**, walking is an adjective because it describes **tour**. But it also acts as a verb because it refers to an action—something someone does.

We call these types of words **verbal adjectives** or **participles**.

A word like **walking** can do different jobs in a sentence; that is, it has different functions.

In the sentence

He went on a walking tour,

walking is an adjective.

In the sentence

Walking is good exercise,

walking is a noun *(see Gerunds p. 5)*.

A walking tour
Adjective

In the sentence

    He is **walking** down the street,

walking is part of the verb.

There are other participles or verbal adjectives:

    a **performing** seal   a **singing** lesson

    a **falling** rock

Verbs

❓ What is a verb? *(See also pp. 80–7)*

A verb is a doing, being or having word.

In the following sentences, ***scratched***, ***was*** and ***have*** are verbs.

    The cat **scratched** my hand.

    My cat **was** angry.

    I **have** a scratch on my hand.

More types of verbs

Doing verbs can be divided into different types: action verbs (***run***, ***swim***, ***ride***); saying verbs (***shout***, ***whisper***); and sensing, thinking and feeling verbs (***wish***, ***wonder***, ***love***). They are all different things you do, so they are all doing verbs.

Being and ***having verbs*** are also called ***relating verbs*** or ***linking verbs*** because they join pieces of information. They do not show action like doing verbs. The most common are the forms of the verbs ***to be***, ***to have*** and ***to seem***. Examples are:

    The plane **is** flying.

    I **have** two sisters.

    They **seem** tired.

Modal verbs

Modal verbs give us information about the amount of possibility or certainty being expressed.

They are usually ***auxiliary verbs*** *(see **auxiliary verbs** below)*. Typical modal verbs are ***might***, ***may*** and ***could*** (low modality or certainty) and ***will***, ***must*** and ***should*** (high modality or certainty), as in:

    I **might** see you there.

    You **must** see that movie.

Negative forms

So far we have talked about verbs in the positive form. We can make them negative. To do this, we add **not**.

>I have not worked hard.

If there is no auxiliary (helping) verb, we have to add **do** or **does** to make the verb negative.

>I do not play football.
>He does not play football.

Negatives can also be contracted.

>I haven't worked hard.
>I don't play football.
>He doesn't play football.

Finite verbs

Verbs can be *finite* or *non-finite*.
Finite verbs have a subject and can stand alone in a clause or sentence without a helping verb.

In the sentence

>The tree crashed to the ground,

crashed is the finite verb and *the tree* is the subject. To find the subject of a finite verb, you ask **Who?** or **What?** before the verb.

What crashed? The answer is *the tree*, so *crashed* is a finite verb. Every clause or sentence must have a finite verb.

The tree crashed to the ground.
Finite verb

Non-finite verbs

Non-finite verbs cannot stand alone and make sense.

To see the movie does not make sense. *To see* is not a finite verb and *to see the movie* is not a sentence.

There are two kinds of non-finite verbs: *infinitives* and *participles*.

Infinitives

The infinitive of a verb has no subject. It is usually preceded by to.

Some examples are:

> to dance   to eat   to hear
>
> to walk   to swim   to stay

An infinitive can appear without **to** as in

> I did not dare ask

instead of

> I did not dare to ask.

Participles

There are two kinds of participles: present participles and past participles.

Present participles

Present participles combine with an **auxiliary** (helping) **verb** to make a complete verb.

> I am walking on the footpath.

The complete verb is **am walking**. The auxiliary verb is **am** (a part of the verb **to be**) and **walking** is the present participle. The present participle is made by adding **-ing** to the infinitive.

INFINITIVE	PRESENT PARTICIPLE
(to) dance	dancing
(to) move	moving
(to) stay	staying
(to) try	trying
(to) walk	walking

I am dancing.
Present participle

Past participles

Past participles also combine with an auxiliary verb to make a complete verb.

> I had walked on the footpath.

The complete verb is **had walked**. The auxiliary verb is **had** and **walked** is the past participle. Except with irregular verbs, such as **be, been; see, seen; do, done**, the past participle is formed by adding **-ed** to the infinitive as in the following examples:

INFINITIVE	PAST PARTICIPLE
(to) dance	danced
(to) move	moved
(to) stay	stayed
(to) try	tried
(to) walk	walked

I have danced.
Past participle

Transitive and intransitive verbs

A **transitive verb has an object. The word 'transitive' means 'to pass over'. The action passes over from the verb to the object.**

In the following sentence, the action passes over from the verb, *sailed*, to the object, *yacht*.

　　The man sailed the yacht.

To find if a verb has an object, you ask **Who?** or **What?** after the verb.

Question: Sailed what? The answer is *yacht*. So *yacht* is the object and the verb is transitive.

An intransitive verb does not have an object. Examples are:

　　The rain stopped.
　　The shop opened at two.

🍎 Agreement in person and number

Finite verbs are limited by or tied to the subject. Therefore they must agree with the subject in person and number.

Person *(See Nouns p. 1, Pronouns p. 6 and agreement above)*

Pronouns have three persons: first person (speaking), second person (spoken to) and third person (spoken about). All nouns are in the third person.

　　I like ice cream. (first person)
　　You like ice cream. (second person)
　　He likes ice cream. (third person)
　　Girls like ice cream. (third person)

The verb changes to *likes* in the third person to agree with the subject.

Irregular verbs like the verb *to be* have more changes.

If the subject is in the first person, the verb must take the first person form.

　　I am on holidays.

If the subject is in the second person, the verb must take the second person form.

　　You are my friend.

If the subject is in the third person, the verb must take the third person form.

　　He is my brother.

Number

Number refers to singular (one) or plural (more than one).

If the subject of a clause or sentence is singular, the verb must be singular; if the subject is plural, the verb must be plural. That is, the verb must agree with the subject in number. For example:

This horse jumps fences.

SINGULAR SUBJECT	SINGULAR VERB	OBJECT
This horse	jumps	fences.

These horses jump fences.

PLURAL SUBJECT	PLURAL VERB	OBJECT
These horses	jump	fences.

The **bird sings**.
Singular subject, singular verb

The **birds sing**.
Plural subject, plural verb

Tense

Tense refers to time and tells us whether the process or action is taking place now (present tense), has taken place (past tense), or will take place some time in the future (future tense).

I **like** school.
[present tense]

My mother **liked** school.
[past tense]

My baby sister **will** like school.
[future tense]

There are several different forms of the present, past and future tenses so we can express a wide range of meanings. These tenses are *simple form*, *continuous form*, *perfect form* and *perfect continuous form*.

The simple form

The simple form consists of short forms of the present, past and future tenses as shown above: *like, liked, will like*.

Another form of the present tense is the timeless present. It means that the action keeps going on, although the verb is in the *simple form*. Examples are:

He **lives** here.
I **play** tennis.

The continuous form

The continuous form tells us that the action or process *is*, *was* or *will be* continuing.

The continuous tenses use the verb *to be* together with the *present participle*.

Present continuous tense

   I am helping my mum.

Past continuous tense

   I was helping my mum last weekend.

Future continuous tense

   I will be helping my mum this weekend.

I am helping my mum.
Present continuous

The perfect form

The perfect form tells us that the event, action or process *is* completed, *was* completed or *will be* completed. The perfect tenses use the verb *to have* with the *past participle*.

Present perfect tense

   He has helped many people.

Past perfect tense

   He had helped a lot of people.

Future perfect tense

   He will have helped many people this year.

The perfect continuous form

The perfect continuous form combines the perfect and the continuous forms in the present, past and future tenses.

Present perfect continuous tense

   She has been helping many people.

Past perfect continuous tense

   She had been helping many people.

Future perfect continuous tense

   She will have been helping many people.

---

shall and will in common usage

In the past when we first used the first person singular or plural personal pronoun (*I* or *we*), shall was used.

> I **shall** be helping.
>
> We **shall** be helping.
>
> If we used second or third person singular or plural personal pronouns (**you**, **he**, **she**, **it**, **they**), **will** was used.
>
> He **will** go shopping on Saturday.
>
> They **will** go to the beach on Sunday.
>
> If we wanted to show emphasis, we used **will** for the first person and **shall** for the second and third person.
>
> I **will** win this race.
>
> They **shall** be caught.
>
> These days, most writers don't make this distinction and seldom use **shall**.

Mood

Mood refers to the way the process or action is expressed by the verb.

There are three moods: ***the indicative mood***, ***the imperative mood*** and ***the subjunctive mood***.

The indicative mood

This is the mood of sentences that ***give facts***.

> The dog **bit** the policeman.

The imperative mood

This is a ***command***.

> **Come** inside and have your tea.

The subjunctive mood

This expresses some action as a ***doubt***, ***possibility*** or ***wish***.

> If your cousin **should come**, he would be welcome.
>
> If I **were** you, I'd go home.

Voice—who is doing the action?

The voice of a verb tells whether the subject does the action or whether something is done to it.

There are two voices, ***active*** and ***passive***.

Active voice

In the active voice, the subject does something to some person or thing.

    John **climbed** the fence.

Climbed is a verb in the active voice because John did something (***climbed***) to something (***the fence***).

Passive voice

In the passive voice, the subject receives the action. The passive voice is made up of a form of the verb ***to be*** plus the ***past participle*** of the main verb.

    The fence **was climbed** by John.

The fence is the subject of the sentence and ***was climbed*** is the verb made up of ***was*** (part of the verb ***to be***) and ***climbed***, the past participle of the verb ***to climb***. It is the subject, ***the fence***, that receives the action.

🍎 More about verbs

The verb to be

The verb to be can show present, past and future tenses.

To be

	SINGULAR	PLURAL	PARTICIPLE
PRESENT	I am you are he, she, it is	we, you, they are	being
PAST	I was you were he, she, it was	we, you, they were	been
FUTURE	I will be you will be he, she, it will be	we, you, they will be	—

The verb ***to be*** can be an ***auxiliary verb*** and with other verbs forms the continuous tenses.

    I **am riding** my bike.

    [present continuous tense]

He **was riding** his bike.
[past continuous tense]

She **will be going** home soon.
[future continuous tense]

Compound and auxiliary verbs

Compound verbs are made up of more than one word. They are made up from auxiliary verbs and non-finite verbs (infinitives or participles). They are also known as verb phrases.

They **are going** to the movies.
John **had been helping** for some weeks.

Some auxiliary verbs that are used to show tenses are:

have	I **have** seen a lion.
be	He **is** looking for his bag.
shall/will	I **will** be finishing work soon.
do	I **do** not see it that way.

Regular and irregular verbs

Most verbs form their tenses in a regular way.

To kick

	SINGULAR	PLURAL	PARTICIPLE
PRESENT	I kick you kick he, she, it kicks	we, you, they kick	kicking
PAST	I kicked you kicked he, she, it kicked	we, you, they kicked	kicked
FUTURE	I will kick you will kick he, she, it will kick	we, you, they will kick	—

The important thing to note is that the past tense and the past participle add **-ed** to the infinitive. This may sometimes be shortened to **-d** or **-t**.

INFINITIVE	PAST TENSE	PAST PARTICIPLE
(to) spell	spelt	spelt

Sometimes the past tense of the verb is the same as the past participle.

INFINITIVE	PAST TENSE	PAST PARTICIPLE
(to) spread	spread	spread

Where this occurs, the verb is said to be a *weak* verb.

Some verbs change their spelling in the past tense and past participle. They are the *strong* verbs. They are also called *irregular* verbs.

INFINITIVE	PAST TENSE	PAST PARTICIPLE
(to) ring	rang	rung

You will know these irregular verbs because you use them often. Listen to what you write and see if it sounds right.

Some common irregular verbs

INFINITIVE	PAST TENSE	PAST PARTICIPLE
arise	arose	arisen
become	became	become
choose	chose	chosen
do	did	done
eat	ate	eaten
fly	flew	flown
give	gave	given
go	went	gone
know	knew	known
lie	lay	lain
ring	rang	rung
speak	spoke	spoken
take	took	taken
wear	wore	worn
write	wrote	written

Important

Don't confuse the past tense with the past participle. It's easy to get it right because the past participle is preceded by a part of another verb, usually the verb *to have*.

The bells **rang** last Sunday.
[past tense]

The bells **have rung** every Sunday this month.
[auxiliary plus past participle]

Verb forms with other parts of speech

Infinitives

Infinitives can act as **nouns**, **adjectives** or **adverbs**.

>To dive is fun.
>[noun]

>She has time to spare.
>[adjective]

>They were walking to exercise.
>[adverb]

Present participles

Present participles can act as nouns and are called **verbal nouns** or **gerunds**. They can also act as adjectives and are called **verbal adjectives**.

>Sailing is always enjoyable.
>[verbal noun or gerund]

>We went on a walking tour.
>[verbal adjective]

We went on a walking tour.
Verbal adjective

Adverbs

❓ What is an adverb? *(See also Adverbial phrases pp. 40, 85, Adverbial clauses pp. 44, 85, Adverbials pp. 87–8 and Adverbial group pp. 87–8)*

Adverbs add meaning to (modify) verbs, adjectives and other adverbs.

Quickly is an adverb in:
>I ran quickly.

Quickly tells **how** I ran.

Very is an adverb in:
>I am a very fast runner.

Very tells **how fast** I ran.

Too is an adverb in:
>You run too quickly for me.

Too tells **how quickly** I ran.

How did you run?
I ran quickly, like this.
Adverb

In the first example, *quickly* adds meaning to the verb, *ran*. In the second, *very* adds meaning to the adjective, *fast*. In the third, *too* adds meaning to the adverb, *quickly*.

Types of adverbs

Adverbs tell how, when, where and why.

They are often called adverbs of *manner*, *time*, *place* and *reason*.

Adverbs of manner

These tell **how** something is done.

I ran quickly.

Adverbs of time

These tell **when** something is done.

I ran yesterday.

Adverbs of place

These tell **where** something is done.

I ran there.

Adverbs of reason

These tell **why** something is done.

Therefore I argue …

I ran there.
Adverb of place, telling where I ran

Other types of adverbs

There are other types of adverbs. You should recognise the following:

Interrogative adverbs

These ask questions.

How are you?

Where did she come from?

Negative adverbs

These make sentences negative.

In the sentence

I do not agree,

not is a negative adverb.

Modal adverbs

Modal adverbs show the amount of probability, certainty or obligation in a sentence.

Yes, **probably**, **possibly**, **certainly** and **definitely** are examples of modal adverbs. They agree or express doubt. (*See also* **Modal adjectives** *p. 17 and* **Modal verbs** *p. 19*)

Numerical adverbs

These tell how often something took place.

>   He called her twice.

Adverbs of degree

Words like **almost**, **hardly**, **enough** and **extremely** tell us **to what extent** something happens. They also tell us **how**, so they are really adverbs of manner, too.

🍎 Important

Remember that adverbs add meaning to verbs, adjectives and other adverbs; not to nouns. If you remember this point, you will always recognise them in sentences and use them well.

–ly and adverbs

Many adverbs end in **-ly**.

>   I can hardly see.
>   She is nearly ten.

Remember, though, that some **-ly** words are adjectives.

>   He was a kindly man.
>   The early bird catches the worm.

It all depends on whether the word adds meaning to a noun or to another part of speech, such as a verb.

🍎 More about adverbs

Adverbs and degree

Like adjectives, adverbs have three degrees of comparison: ***positive***, ***comparative*** and ***superlative***, and they use the same endings to show them.

POSITIVE	COMPARATIVE	SUPERLATIVE
sang loudly	sang more loudly	sang most loudly

Some adverbs look like adjectives in positive, comparative and superlative forms. You will know they are adverbs because they add meaning to verbs, adjectives and other adverbs.

Examples are:

| hard | harder | hardest |
| long | longer | longest |

He hit the ball hard.
Adverb of manner
Positive degree

A few adverbs form degrees of comparison in an irregular way.

good	better	best
much	more	most
badly	worse	worst

good   better   best

Prepositions

What is a preposition?

Prepositions show relationships between nouns or pronouns and other words.

Preposition means 'placed in front', so they are usually found in front of nouns or pronouns.

in the soup
near them

In these phrases, *in* and *near* are prepositions: *in* is related to **soup**; *near* is related to **them**.

Prepositions are said to govern nouns or pronouns in the objective case. Prepositions are usually short words, although some, like **underneath**, are long. Here are 20 common prepositions. There are many more.

across	beneath	into	over	before
after	between	like	past	in
among	during	near	to	on
around	from	of	up	with

Across the sea

Up the hill

Across and **up** are prepositions.

🍎 More about prepositions

Special prepositions

Some nouns, adjectives and verbs are followed by particular prepositions.
We say:

✅ The team ran **onto** the field.

Not

❌ The team ran ~~into~~ the field.

You know which preposition to use in most cases because it sounds right when you say it. We are pleased **with** things; we rely **on** things and we bring them **under** control.

Some need special attention.

We say:

✅ different **from**	✅ **between** two	✅ **among** three (or more)
Not	Not	Not
❌ different ~~to~~	❌ ~~among~~ two	❌ ~~between~~ three (or more)
❌ different ~~than~~		

Prepositions and adverbs

It is important not to confuse adverbs with prepositions.

They may look exactly the same. You will know the difference because of the way the word is used.

In

    I fell **down**,

down is an adverb of place; it tells *where I fell*.

In

    I rowed **down** the river,

down is a preposition governing *river* in the objective case.

Another useful point is that the preposition usually has a noun or pronoun after it.

33

I fell down.
[adverb]

I rowed down the river.
[preposition]

Conjunctions

What is a conjunction? *(See Cohesion p. 54 and Connectives p. 55)*

A **conjunction** is a joining word.

The bat hit the ball and the ball hit me.

Coordinate conjunctions

Conjunctions form a link between one word and another. The words they join are usually the same or a similar part of speech. These linking words are called **coordinate conjunctions**.

The common coordinate conjunctions are:

and   but   for   nor   or   so   yet

wet and cold

tired but happy

apple or pear

smoothly yet efficiently

Coordinate conjunctions can also join larger groups of words together, such as compound words and phrases.

Mary Jones and John Smith

in the sea and on a surfboard

Coordinate conjunctions can also join sentences together.

That is his book. That is her book.

That is his book and that is her book.

Correlative conjunctions

Some conjunctions exist in pairs. These conjunctions are called **correlative conjunctions**.

The most common correlative conjunctions are:

both … and   either … or

neither … nor   not only … but also

whether … or   not … but

as … as

The batsman was not only stumped but also caught.

Neither Alberto **nor** Maria is in my class.

Both James and Sarah left **as** soon **as** John arrived.

Subordinate conjunctions

Some conjunctions join parts of sentences called clauses. *(See also* **Clauses** *pp. 43–6)*

I want to be a plumber **when** I grow up.

This example contains two clauses: ***I want to be a plumber*** is the main part of the sentence, and ***when I grow up*** tells us when the person wants this to happen.

For the sentence to make sense, ***when I grow up*** depends on ***I want to be a plumber***. We say that ***when I grow up*** is subordinate to ***I want to be a plumber***. The word that joins these two parts of the sentence (***when***) is called a ***subordinate conjunction***.

You will learn more about subordinate conjunctions when you read the chapter on clauses.

The most common subordinate conjunctions are:

after	before	though	whenever
although	once	unless	where
as	since	until	wherever
because	than	when	while

Some more examples

I was late for school **because** I missed the bus.

I'm all right **once** I get started.

I can't get into the house **until** Mum comes home.

This is the place **where** I go to school.

I do my homework while Dad is cooking tea.
While is a subordinate conjunction.

35

Articles

What is an article? *(See also Determiners p. 88)*

There are only three articles: **the**, **a**, and **an**.

They describe nouns and are adjectives of a special kind.

The Pacific Ocean

A river

An ocean

Definite article

The is the definite article. It is called definite because it refers to a particular thing or things.

The train is coming.
The apples are in the box.

Indefinite article

A and an are indefinite articles. These articles do not refer to particular things.

It's cold, so wear a coat.
An ant is strong for its size.

The *a* might mean any number of coats, not a special one; the *an* refers to all ants, not a particular or definite one.

a is used in front of a consonant	a coat
an is used in front of a vowel	an ant

Interjections

❓ What is an interjection?

Interjections are words that interrupt the flow of conversation.

They express a strong feeling about something.

Interjections are usually followed by an exclamation mark.

Taste this!

I was running along when, ouch! I tripped over a rock.

There are many other interjections. Here are some:
  Ow!
  Ah!
  Eeek!
  Oops!
  Ooo!
  Yow!
  Wow!

Parsing

The word **parsing** comes from the Latin word **pars** meaning 'part'. When you parse a sentence you say what you know about each part of speech in it; you identify what each word is doing. That is, you state its function.

Here is an example of parsing:

The hungry tiger watched them closely.
A sentence for parsing

- Name each part of speech in the sentence.

ARTICLE	ADJECTIVE	NOUN	VERB	PRONOUN	ADVERB
The	hungry	tiger	watched	them	closely.

- Say what you know about each part of speech.

The	definite article
hungry	descriptive adjective qualifying the noun **tiger**
tiger	common noun, third person; singular number; common gender (masculine or feminine); nominative case, subject of the verb **watched**
watched	transitive, finite verb; third person, singular number to agree with its subject, **tiger**; past tense, indicative mood, active voice
them	personal pronoun; third person; plural number; common gender; objective case after the verb **watched**
closely	adverb of manner, modifying the verb **watched**

Modern teachers would not need to parse a whole sentence because they are usually more interested in a particular word and how it works or how it fits into bigger parts of a sentence. Nevertheless, parsing helps us to use words correctly because we understand the function of each part of speech.

PHRASE LEVEL

Phrases

What is a phrase?

A **phrase** is a group of words that has no finite verb.

It is not a complete message by itself.

> I know that boy with red hair.

The words **with red hair** form a phrase that tells us more about the noun **boy**.

Different types of phrases

Phrases can do the work of different parts of speech.

Adjectival phrases

Phrases that do the work of adjectives are called adjectival phrases. Like adjectives, they add meaning to, describe or modify nouns or pronouns.

> Elena is the girl in the blue jeans.

The phrase *in the blue jeans* describes the noun **girl** and so is an adjectival phrase. Adjectival phrases can begin in different ways.

Beginning with a preposition

They may begin with a preposition.

> Elena is the girl in the blue jeans.

The adjectival phrase *in the blue jeans* begins with the preposition *in* and describes the noun **girl**.

Beginning with a present participle

> The children, wearing their hats, played in the sun.

The adjectival phrase *wearing their hats* begins with the present participle *wearing* and modifies the noun **children**.

Beginning with a past participle

> I felt sorry for the girls locked in the lavatory.

The adjectival phrase *locked in the lavatory* begins with the past participle *locked* and modifies the noun **girls**.

Beginning with an infinitive

>He got the message *to be quiet*.

The adjectival phrase **to be quiet** begins with an infinitive **to be** and modifies the noun **message**.

Adverbial phrases

Phrases that do the work of adverbs are called adverbial phrases. Like adverbs, they add meaning to or modify the action of verbs. They tell how, when, where or why the action takes place.

Adverbs can also modify adjectives and other adverbs.

>He cut the rope *with a single slash*.

The phrase **with a single slash** modifies the verb **cut**. It tells **how** the rope was cut, so it is an adverbial phrase.

Adverbial phrases may also begin in different ways. They begin with a preposition or an infinitive.

>I sat *in the park*.

>I sat down *to have a rest*.

There are four kinds of adverbial phrases. They are:

- adverbial phrases of *manner* (how)
- adverbial phrases of *time* (when)
- adverbial phrases of *place* (where)
- adverbial phrases of *reason* (why).

Adverbial phrases of manner

>The dog was barking *in a threatening way*.

The adverbial phrase of manner is **in a threatening way**. It tells **how** about the verb **was barking**.

Adverbial phrases of time

>*Over the weekend*, all the family play sport.

The adverbial phrase of time is **over the weekend**. It tells **when** about the verb **play**.

Adverbial phrases of place

>We often eat our lunch *on the school bus*.

The adverbial phrase of place is **on the school bus**. It tells **where** about the verb **eat**.

Adverbial phrases of reason (See also **Causality** p. 88)

We lost the game because of the muddy ground.

The adverbial phrase of reason is **because of the muddy ground**. It tells **why** about the verb **lost**.

Adverbial phrases of reason beginning with an infinitive

They played hard to win the game.

The adverbial phrase of reason is **to win the game**. It tells **why** about the verb **played**. The phrase begins with the infinitive **to win**.

Noun phrases

Phrases that do the work of a noun are called noun phrases.

A noun phrase stands in place of a noun.

Playing football can be dangerous.

The phrase **playing football** stands for a noun, so it is a noun phrase.

Noun phrases usually begin with a gerund (verbal noun). *(See **Gerunds (verbal nouns)** p. 5)*

Noun phrases as the subject of the sentence

Patting stray dogs is very silly.

If you ask the question **What is?**, the answer will be **patting stray dogs**.

It is a noun phrase because it acts like a noun, is the subject of the sentence and begins with the gerund (verbal noun) patting.

Noun phrases as the object of the sentence

I love eating baked beans.

If you ask the question **I love what?**, the answer will be **eating baked beans**.

It is a noun phrase because it acts like a noun, is the object of the sentence and begins with the gerund eating.

🍎 More about phrases

Sometimes phrases are described by the part of speech they begin with, rather than the job they do in the sentence. If we look at them in this way, we could describe phrases as **prepositional phrases** or **verbal phrases**.

Prepositional phrases always begin with a preposition.

Verbal phrases can be subdivided into:

- **participial phrases**, which begin with either a present or a past participle
- **gerund phrases**, which begin with a gerund
- **infinitive phrases**, which begin with an infinitive.

Whatever a phrase begins with, it is the job the phrase does that is most important. So, when a phrase has been identified (i.e. a group of words without a finite verb), then it is important to ask whether it is doing its job as:

- an **adjective** (adds meaning to, describes or modifies a noun);
- an **adverb** (adds meaning to or modifies a verb, an adjective or another adverb); or
- a **noun** (when you can answer *something* to the question *What?*).

CLAUSE LEVEL
Clauses

❓ What is a clause? *(See also Groups p. 85 and Theme and rheme p. 86)*

A **clause** is a group of words that contains a finite verb and its subject.

    Fish swim

is a clause. **Swim** is the finite verb and **fish** is the subject.

Clauses may have more words as well.

    Fish swim in the sea

is also a clause.

The principal clause *(See also Independent clause p. 86)*

The **principal clause** is a clause that makes sense by itself. It can stand alone.

    Fish swim

is a principal clause. So is

    Fish swim in the sea.

These clauses make sense by themselves.

Because principal clauses make sense by themselves, they can also be sentences. **Fish swim** is a sentence, and so is **Fish swim in the sea**.

Some sentences, however, can contain two or more principal clauses. These clauses are joined by coordinate conjunctions.

    <u>Fish swim in the sea</u> and <u>cows walk on the land</u>.

The subordinate clause *(See also Dependent clause and Embedded clause p. 87)*

The **subordinate clause** adds meaning to the principal clause. It is called a subordinate clause because it is dependent of the principal clause. It cannot exist by itself; it needs the principal clause.

    Fish swim in the sea │because they cannot walk on the land.│

The subordinate clause in this sentence is *because they cannot walk on the land*.

I think, therefore I am.
Subordinate clause

Recognising principal and subordinate clauses

It is usually easy to recognise principal and subordinate clauses in sentences. Here are some examples. The principal clauses are underlined and the subordinate clauses are in a box.

<u>I saw him</u> when I came in.
<u>This is the boy</u> who won the race.
<u>We know</u> that the sky is blue.

Watch out for principal clauses that are in two parts.

<u>The big red car,</u> which I drove, <u>won the race</u>.

In this sentence, the principal clause is **The big red car won the race**.

Types of subordinate clauses

Subordinate clauses are described by the same name as the parts of speech that could take their place. They have the same work to do.

Adverbial clauses

Adverbial clauses do the work of adverbs.

I ate my breakfast after I had a shower.

After I had a shower tells when I ate my breakfast, so it does the work of an adverb. It is an *adverbial clause*.

Like adverbs, there are adverbial clauses of **manner**, **time**, **place** and **reason**.

They tell **how**, **when**, **where** and **why**.

YNT may do as you please.
[*how*: manner]

We cheered when they arrived.
[*when*: time]

They fish where the water is deep.
[*where*: place]

I'll have strawberry because it is my favourite.
[*why*: reason]

Other types of adverbial clauses are:

Comparison

It is not as valuable as it looks.

Concession

I fed the dog although it tried to bite me.

Condition

    I will meet him if he is on time.

Degree or comparison

    The girl could run as fast as a hare.

Purpose

    They went to the beach so they could surf.

Result

    He ran so fast that he won the race.

Adverbial clauses begin with **subordinate conjunctions**. Some subordinate conjunctions are:

after	although	as	because
since	until	when	while

(See also Causality p. 88)

Adjectival clauses

Adjectival clauses do the work of adjectives; they add meaning to nouns.

    This is the cat that killed the rat.

That killed the rat is an **adjectival clause** qualifying *cat*. The word *cat* is the antecedent. The word *that*, which begins the adjectival clause, is a **relative pronoun**.

    The relative pronouns are:
    who   whom   which   that

    Another example of an adjectival clause is:
    He spoke to the woman who was watching the cricket.

    Be careful of adjectival clauses like these:
    The snow, which fell all night, was very deep.
    [The principal clause is in two parts.]

    This is the place where we will have lunch.
    [*Where* means 'at which' and the clause is describing the noun *place*.]

(See Embedded clause p. 88)

Noun clauses

Noun clauses do the work of nouns.

They can be either the subject or object of a verb, as in:

    What they saw was amazing.

What they saw is a **noun clause**, the subject of *was*.

I know that the apples are juicy.

That the apples are juicy is a noun clause, the object of **know**.

If a noun clause comes after a part of the verb **to be**, it is said to be the **complement** of the verb. The verbs **seem**, **become**, **remain**, **look** and **appear** also take complements.

That is what I ordered.

What I ordered is a noun clause, complement of the verb *is*.

On some occasions, a noun clause can be the object of a preposition.

I sold the book for what it was worth.

What it was worth is a noun clause, the object of the preposition **for**.

🍎 A point to notice

Noun clauses are often introduced by **that**.

I saw that the ship had arrived.

Sometimes **that** is omitted.

I told him the cake was cooked.

The cake was cooked is a noun clause, the object of **told**.

Noun clauses can be introduced by other words as well. Just remember that the type of clause depends on the job or function the clause has in the sentence.

I know where the dog is hiding.

Where the dog is hiding is a noun clause, the object of **know**.

I told him who won the prize.

Who won the prize is a noun clause, the object of **told**.

SENTENCE LEVEL

Sentences

❓ What is a sentence? *(See also Clause complex p. 88)*

A **sentence** is a group of words that contains a finite verb and has a complete meaning.

The girls played netball.

There are different forms of the sentence.

Statement

I like playing netball.

Question

Is Rachel home?

Command

Come over here at once.

Exclamation

You're out!

Every sentence has at least one *finite verb*—a verb that has a subject.

The dog chased the cat.

The verb is **chased** and it is *finite* because **the dog** is the subject. The rest of the sentence, ***chased the cat***, is called the ***predicate***.

There are different kinds of sentences:

- simple sentences
- compound (combined) sentences
- complex sentences.

**The cat chased the dog.
Statement**

Simple sentences

A **simple sentence** has a subject and a predicate. It has a finite verb, which is the predicate or part of the predicate.

I watched.

FINITE VERB   watched
SUBJECT   I
PREDICATE   watched

I like playing netball.

FINITE VERB   like
SUBJECT   I
PREDICATE   like playing netball

These simple sentences have one main clause in each case. It is called a *principal* or *independent clause*.

Compound (combined) sentences

Sometimes two or more principal clauses are joined by a coordinate conjunction to form a compound sentence.

The cat ran and the dog chased after it.

1ST FINITE VERB   ran
SUBJECT   The cat
PREDICATE   ran
PRINCIPAL CLAUSE   The cat ran
COORDINATE CONJUNCTION   and
2ND FINITE VERB   chased
SUBJECT   the dog
PREDICATE   chased after it
PRINCIPAL CLAUSE   the dog chased after it

This compound sentence has two principal clauses. They are:

the cat ran

the dog chased after it

In the following compound sentences, the finite verbs are in blue and the principal clauses are underlined.

Dad mowed the lawn and Mum weeded the garden.

John played cricket and Anna played tennis.

The phone rang but no-one answered it.

Complex sentences

Complex sentences have a principal clause and another clause, which depends on that principal clause. This dependent clause is called a subordinate clause and begins with a subordinate conjunction or a relative pronoun. *(See Clause level pp. 43–6)*

The cat knew when it was in danger.

1ST FINITE VERB	knew
SUBJECT	The cat
PREDICATE	knew
PRINCIPAL CLAUSE	The cat knew
SUBORDINATE CONJUNCTION	when
2ND FINITE VERB	was
SUBJECT	it
PREDICATE	was in danger
SUBORDINATE CLAUSE	when it was in danger

In the following complex sentences, the finite verbs are in blue. The principal clause is underlined and the subordinate clause is in a box.

The car was very old so Grandma sold it.

When baby James goes to sleep, I will have my meal.

The pen, which I was given for my birthday, was stolen.

Compound/complex sentences

Some sentences can be both compound and complex.

She went running and took her dog, which was a Labrador.

When I finish school, I am going to retire.
Complex sentence

More about sentences

Understood subjects

Some sentences don't seem to have a subject.

Go away!

This sentence is a command. The verb is **go**. When we ask **who** or **what** in front of the verb, we don't seem to get an answer.

When we say **Go away**! we are referring to **you**, even though the word is not written. When this occurs, we say **you** is understood, i.e. the sentence is really saying,

(You) go away!

49

As we have now found the subject, we can say that the verb *go* is a finite verb because it has a subject.

The following sentences have the subject understood.

> Throw that away!
> [subject: you]

> Help!
> [subject: you]

Punctuating sentences

The four forms of the sentence are **statement**, **question**, **command** and **exclamation**.

All sentences begin with a **capital letter**.

> We are going on a holiday. We're going to the Barrier Reef.

Statements end with a full stop.

> She is my friend.

Questions end with a question mark.

> Is Alanna still my friend?

Commands usually end with a full stop.

> Get away from that mud.

Exclamations end with an exclamation mark.

> You're out!

Commas are important in sentences. They help to make the meaning clearer and can change it. Notice the difference in meaning between these two sentences:

> I read the books that I liked.
> I read the books, which I liked.

The first sentence means that I read only the books that I liked (and no others). The second sentence means that I read (all) the books and I liked them.

*(See **Restrictive clauses** p. 89)*

Analysis of sentences

Finding and naming the clauses in sentences is called **analysis**. Analysis is saying what you know about each clause. It often goes with **parsing** *(see p. 38)*, which is saying what you know about each part of speech in a sentence.

Although modern teachers would not analyse sentences completely, analysis tells you how many clauses there will be in the sentence or passage. Following is an example. Begin by underlining the finite verbs:

I saw the whale and I saw the calf. The whale, which was very large, was swimming slowly. I knew that the calf was nearby, because they always swam together.

PRINCIPAL CLAUSE	I saw the whale
PRINCIPAL CLAUSE	I saw the calf
PRINCIPAL CLAUSE	The whale was swimming slowly
ADJECTIVAL CLAUSE	which was very large

(qualifying *whale*)

PRINCIPAL CLAUSE	I knew
NOUN CLAUSE	that the calf was nearby

(object of *knew*)

ADVERBIAL CLAUSE OF REASON	because they always swam together

(modifying *was*)

I saw the whale.
Principal clause

I saw the calf.
Principal clause

TEXT LEVEL

Traditional and functional grammar

Grammar at text level in modern traditional grammar takes on many of the insights of functional grammar *(see pp. 57–89)*. It is the point where the two grammars meet in modern school syllabuses.

🍎 Text level structure

The text, whether spoken or written, goes beyond word level, phrase/group level and sentence level. Text level refers to the structure (make-up) of a particular text type such as a narrative or a procedure, to the formation of paragraphs and the way that the whole text holds together or coheres. *(See **Cohesion** p. 54)*

When we understand how a text is put together, and how each one is different in its structure, we are better able to understand the text and write another one like it.

To understand the grammar of a whole text we need to look at the words, phrases, clauses and sentences in a text as well.

🍎 Text differences

Text types are very different from one another *(see pp. 58–77)*. For instance, a ***narrative***, a literary text type, tells a story and contains different characters. It is made up of an orientation that sets up the scene of the story, then the story itself, with its complication and the final resolution. In a narrative there are many different examples of grammar at the various levels: proper nouns, action verbs, different clauses, sentence types and a host of other different grammatical features.

A ***procedure*** is a factual text type, not a literary one. It contains a goal, such as 'how to make muffins', a list of the things needed, then the steps or instructions that show the reader what to do. In a procedure you will find commands, action verbs, adverbial phrases and connectives such as ***first*** and ***next***.

Paragraphs

Written texts can be divided into ***paragraphs***.

Paragraphs are little 'chunks' or bundles of information that deal with a main idea or ideas in a text and usually consist of a number of sentences. Each paragraph usually has a topic sentence that pinpoints the main idea.

Here is an example of paragraphs in an exposition.

Nuts are good for you

Paragraph 1 **Nuts are good for you.** They are a rich source of protein and other important nutrients. These include unsaturated fats, amino acids, vitamins and potassium. However, there is a wrong way and a right way to eat nuts.

Topic sentence (Nuts are good for you)

Paragraph 2 **Here is the wrong way: eating nuts as an extra to your usual intake of meals and snacks will make you put on weight.** It could add another five kilos or more to your body weight over a year.

Topic sentence (Here is the wrong way ...)

Paragraph 3 **Here is the right way: eat nuts instead of chips or sweets for a snack.** Include nuts as part of your usual lunch and eat them instead of meat for your main meal. They make delicious dishes. Nuts are good for you, there's no doubt.

Topic sentence (Here is the right way ...)

Nuts are good for you.
Topic sentence

The topic sentence

The topic sentence is usually at the beginning of a paragraph. It summarises the main idea.

The remainder of the paragraph gives the points that support it (in the case of an exposition or discussion, as in 'Nuts are good for you').

Theme (See **Theme and rheme** p. 86)

The theme of a clause directs the flow of information and places focus on the idea that is to be developed. It is a signal for the reader.

In the example on p. 53, the theme of the first sentence is **nuts** and the rheme is the rest of the clause. The emphasis is on **nuts** as it is first.

Here are some examples of theme patterns in different text types:

Narrative	Once upon a time …
Exposition	Secondly, it is argued …
Procedure	Slice … stir …
Recount	Afterwards we …

Once upon a time …
Narrative

Cohesion (See p. 82)

Cohesion forms links (cohesive ties) that hold the text together.

There are many ways the links are formed. They include reference ties, substitution, conjunctions, and others. *(See **Functional grammar** pp. 57–89)* All of the devices that make the text hold together (cohere) are important and make the text an interconnected whole.

🍎 Further text links

Other text links are formed by words that have association with one another.

Repetition

Repetition forms links through the repeating of words or groups of words.

> **Kangaroos** are marsupials. **Kangaroos** carry their young in pouches. **Kangaroos** move by …
>
> **In the rainforest** you will find dense vegetation. **In the rainforest** animal life is …

Synonyms

Synonyms are words that have the same or similar meaning, such as laugh and chuckle; leap and jump; sleep and slumber.

Antonyms

Antonyms are words that have opposite meanings, such as hot and cold; fast and slow; wet and dry.

Sometimes groups of words contrast with one another: ***brightly polished silver*** and ***dull, corroded brass***.

Collocation (See p. 88)

Collocation is a general, wider term used for words that usually go together (co-locate), such as **kitchen, bedroom, bathroom, sitting room, rumpus room, study**. They may include some of the linking devices outlined above or others such as word sets or clusters.

Word sets, chains, word families

(a) Whole to part

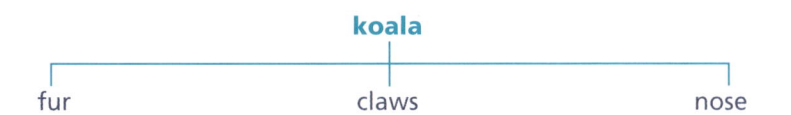

koala
- fur
- claws
- nose

(b) Class to sub-class

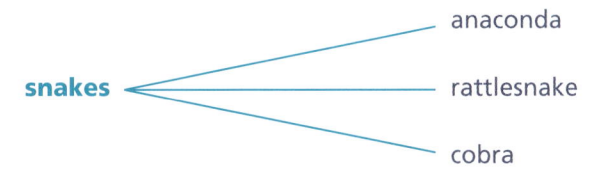

snakes
- anaconda
- rattlesnake
- cobra

(c) Creature and attributes

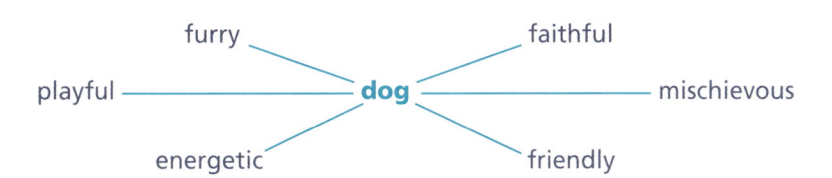

dog
- furry
- faithful
- playful
- mischievous
- energetic
- friendly

Connectives (See pp. 74, 75)

Connectives are words or groups of words that give the reader signposts for showing how the text is developing and what might come next.

Some connectives are:

Showing time	now, afterwards
Clarifying	for example, for instance
Result	so, therefore, because of this
Keeping ideas in order	first, to start with
New information	in addition, furthermore, also
Conditions apply	however, despite this, besides

Note: Conjunctions join clauses within sentences.

Connectives form links between sentences and longer pieces of text.

Traditional and functional grammar

55

🍎 Dialogue patterns

Texts are also held together by dialogue patterns. These differ depending on the register, the way a text changes with relation to the topic, the people involved and the form of language—whether the text is written or spoken. An example of differences in dialogue pattern is illustrated by the two texts on p. 78. *(See Register p. 77)*

🍎 Watch out for homonyms

Homonyms are words that look the same or sound the same (or both) and have different meanings *(see pp. 117–141 for a further explanation and a list of common homonyms).*

If we use the wrong word in reading or writing, the meaning of the whole text may break down. The correct homonyms make links in the text. Think of the differences in meaning between the following pairs of homonyms:

row (row a boat)	row (make a noise)
eight (number)	ate (food)
dear (loved, expensive)	deer (animal)
bark (of a tree)	bark (sound made by a dog)

Note: Words that look the same are called ***homographs*** (same spelling).
Words that sound the same are called ***homophones*** (same sound).

He is my dear friend.
Is this what you really mean?

FUNCTIONAL GRAMMAR

Introduction

Functional grammar helps us look more closely at the way language works, particularly beyond the level of the sentence. It places emphasis on the purpose for which a text is written.

The purpose determines the text structure. When we look closely at different text structures and the grammatical features that are a defining part of those structures, we are studying the genres or text types. For example, if a piece of writing is a report, its structure and grammatical features are very different from that of a narrative.

We will consider five different literary text types, including poetry. Seven factual text types will also be studied. It is important to remember that text types can be both oral and written. You can tell a story or you can write a story, for example. Both are narratives and will contain similar structural and grammatical features. There may also be many forms of the narrative, for example, narrative poems and myths and legends. Narratives may also be explored visually through a series of pictures or the stimulus of one picture.

While we can divide text types into broad categories, in many ways these categories are arbitrary. Overlap is inevitable when grouping and defining text types. Also, any text may contain more than one text type. A narrative may contain a description and/or an explanation and/or an exposition and/or other text types.

Thus, text types should not be restricted to the printed word, and experience in other modes of communication is an important component in understanding the complex task of receiving and transmitting ideas.

Genres or text types

The following text types will be examined:

Literary text: Narrative, literary recount, literary description, literary review and poetry. Poetry is included as a text type although some regard this form as a channel of communication for different text types.

Factual text: Factual description, information report, procedure (and procedural recount), factual recount, explanation, exposition and discussion.

🍎 Literary texts

Narrative

Social purpose: A narrative tells a story by constructing a pattern of events. The events may have an outcome that the reader or listener finds unexpected or that may raise a problem. A narrative entertains because it stimulates creative thinking, and it instructs because it makes the reader or listener think and feel about the characters and happenings in the story. Examples of narratives are ***The Lord of the Rings*** by J.R.R. Tolkien, ***Charlotte's Web*** by E.B. White, ***Bridge to Terabithia*** by Katherine Paterson and ***Watership Down*** by Richard Adams. Narratives can be long or short and may be written in prose or verse. Examples of verse narratives are ***The Highwayman*** by Alfred Noyes or ***Mulga Bill*** and ***The Man from Snowy River*** by A.B. Paterson.

Structure: A narrative is usually made up of an orientation, a complication and a resolution, in which the problems are usually worked out. Sometimes a narrative finishes with a comment by the author. This is called a coda.

Grammatical features:

- the use of particular nouns that refer to or describe the characters or events
- the use of adjectives and adjectival phrases and/or clauses that build up a description of the parts of the story
- the use of past tense action verbs
- the use of saying and thinking verbs to indicate what a character is feeling, thinking or saying
- the use of adverbs and adverbial phrases and/or clauses to locate where or when the action took place
- the use of conjunctions and time connectives to show the sequence of events.

Theseus and the Minotaur

Structure	Text	Some language features
Orientation	The Minotaur was a terrifying monster with the head and shoulders of a bull and the body of a man. It lived in the palace of King Minos of Crete and ate the flesh of humans. King Minos had built a	particular nouns

	labyrinth or maze made of stone to keep the Minotaur prisoner. The labyrinth was so **complicated** that no one who entered it had ever found their way out again.	— *particular noun*
Complication	King Minos **had thought** up a cruel plan for feeding the Minotaur. Every year King Minos made **King Aegeus** of Athens send **seven young** men and **seven young** women to Crete to be fed to the Minotaur. Every year this caused much grieving amongst the people of Athens.	— *thinking verb* — *particular noun* — *adjectivals*
Series of events	One year, Theseus, the son of King Aegeus, **said** he would take the place of one of the young people and find a way to kill the Minotaur. The King and Queen and all the other mothers and fathers **sadly** waved the young people goodbye as they set sail for Crete. When the seven men and women arrived on Crete they were immediately taken to the palace. There, King Minos's beautiful daughter, Ariadne, saw Theseus and **instantly** fell in love with him. She decided to help him kill the monster.	— *saying verb* — *adverbials*
	Ariadne **arranged** to meet Theseus secretly at the entrance to the labyrinth. When they met she gave him a sword and a ball of silken thread. "Be very careful," she **warned** him. "The labyrinth is as dangerous as the Minotaur."	— *past tense action verb* — *saying verb*
	Theseus, [**who was as clever as he was handsome and brave**], **tied** one end of the	— *adjectival clause* — *past tense action verb*

Genres or text types

59

thread to a rock at the entrance of the labyrinth. **As he felt his way along the dark tunnels**, he unrolled the thread until eventually he came to a place scattered with skulls and bones.

— *adverbial clause*

Suddenly, Theseus heard a deafening roar and quickly *turned* around. **Luckily** he dodged the fearsome horns of the Minotaur *just in time*. **Swiftly**, he swung his sword and with enormous strength struck the horrible beast across the back. Then he stood still and waited and listened. Before long he heard an even louder roar. The Minotaur had only been wounded **by the first blow** and now it attacked *again*. This time Theseus **plunged** his sword straight into the Minotaur's heart. Now there was only silence **in the labyrinth**.

— *past tense action verb*

— *adverbials*

Resolution — Theseus *recovered* his breath and followed the thread back to the entrance where Ariadne was nervously waiting for him. He took her aboard his ship and they sailed away with the young Athenian men and women he had saved. Theseus became a hero and he and Ariadne *were married* **with King Aegeus's blessing**.

— *past tense action verbs*

— *adverbial*

Literary recount

Social purpose: A literary recount retells the sequence of events as they happened in a literary context and enables the author to make a judgment about those events and/or the characters. Its purpose is to give an entertaining and personal rendition of events. It may be either oral or written and the narrative may be in the form of prose or verse.

Examples are the retelling of tales of the exploits of mythical heroes such as Jason, Theseus and Hercules. Others are the recounts of the experiences of famous people like Sir Edmund Hillary's historic climb of Mt Everest or the exploits of the young man from Snowy River.

Structure: Literary recount is made up of an introduction and a record of events that may contain personal comments by the author. These comments may seek to evaluate or judge events or the behaviour of the characters. This is usually followed by a reorientation that rounds off the text by incorporating comments and attitudes that the author now holds about the events or the characters.

Grammatical features:

- the use of nouns and pronouns to identify the characters of the story
- the use of adjectives and adjectival phrases (adjectivals) and/or adjectival clauses that describe the nouns and pronouns
- the use of action verbs that refer to the events
- the use of past tense verbs to give a sense of the writer's or storyteller's time
- the use of adverbs and adverbial phrases (adverbials) and/or adverbial clauses that indicate place and time
- the use of conjunctions and connectives to sequence the events.

A literary recount has the same structure and common grammatical features as a factual text, whose purpose is to recount events or procedures. *(See Factual recount pp. 70–1 for an example of text and a listing of structural and language features)*

Literary description

Social purpose: A literary description describes in literary terms a particular thing, such as a scene, an animal, a person or something that happened in nature. The emphasis is on individual things, not on a general class of things. A literary description can also be imaginative or impressionistic.

A literary description can be part of a narrative or another literary text. It makes us look closely at a thing to see what it is really like. Examples are the descriptions of the hobbit's hole at the beginning of **The Hobbit** by J.R.R. Tolkien, nineteenth-century Sydney in **Playing Beatie Bow** by Ruth Park, the Coorong at the beginning of **Storm Boy** by Colin Thiele and the animals in **The Wind in the Willows** by Kenneth Grahame.

Structure: A literary description is made up of an introduction and a description and may end with a personal evaluation by the author. This can take the form of a concluding comment.

Grammatical features:

- the use of particular nouns identified from the literary text
- the use of detailed noun groups to provide more information about a particular person or thing
- the use of adjectives and adjectival phrases (adjectivals) and/or adjectival clauses that function to give an opinion, a factual description or the amount or numerical number (quantity), or to classify the noun
- the use of relating verbs and thinking and feeling verbs to give the author's personal viewpoint, and action verbs to describe the character's behaviour
- the use of adverbs and adverbial phrases (adverbials) and/or adverbial clauses that provide information about the character's behaviour
- the use of figurative language such as metaphors to enhance meaning.

A literary description has the same structure and common language features as a factual description *(see p. 67)*, whose purpose is to focus attention on the characteristic features of a particular thing. Consequently, when a student engages with a literary text, the result can be a powerful and evocative experience for the reader/listener. It could assist understanding by enabling that person to identify with and more perceptively understand both place and character. Literary observation is the prelude to literary description.

Wongadilla

Structure	Text	Some language features
Introduction and descriptive features	Wongadilla is [one knot in a tangle of spurs and ridges]. You would say it is much like other sheep-runs nearby but Charlie claims it is greener. Its steepest, sharpest height is called 'the mountain' but really it is [a clump of high and higher tops melted together in one]. There are green places high and low and slopes of tall grass the colour of moonlight; shade trees everywhere, and a patch or two of scrub, and rock [breaking through in the steepest places].	metaphor particular noun relating verbs detailed noun group adjectival

Descriptive features	Halfway down its looming height, the mountain spreads a broad lap, and from there, throws out three ridges into the flat between it and the opposite mountain. One of these is … **like a long arm running out from under its rocky shoulder**. This ridge is covered in forest and lies half in Wongadilla and half outside it; [**Charlie's boundary fence, running down the mountain**], cuts [**across this ridge and through the forest**], and takes in the flat below. The flat spreads wide [**between this ridge and the other two**], [**like the space between your thumb and your first two fingers**].	— *simile* — *detailed noun group* — *adverbials* — *simile*
	The other two ridges lie close together, holding between them a narrow, deep gully where the creek runs down to the river. Where they join the mountain is **the round green swelling of a hill**, and behind this is a hollow **that is always green with a glint**. This **is** the swamp. When you come to it, hidden on the side of the mountain and halfway up to the crest of the wind, then you begin to know Wongadilla.	— *detailed noun group* — *relating verb* — *adjectival clause*
Concluding comment	If you go into the swamp you feel [**no squish of mud but rough clean water-couch springing under your toes**]. Rafts of pink-tipped weed **drift** with the wind, drawing its pattern in lines on the water. Jelly-froth rafts of frog-spawn **are moored**	— *detailed noun group* — *action verbs*

Genres or text types

63

Functional grammar

to tufts of bull-grass, for the swamp is always loud with the creaking and hiccupping of frogs. There are [rootled-out snuffed-up holes] [where a wombat was feeding]—a tuft of clean mauve fur left by a swamp-wallaby—it is like seeing a door close as someone slips away.

- adjectival
- relating verbs
- detailed noun groups
- adjectival clause
- adverbial clause

(Patricia Wrightson, from *The Nargun and the Stars*)

Literary review

Social purpose: A literary review is a response to a text. This response may summarise and/or analyse the appeal and value of that text to the assumed reader. A review can be either oral or written in form. Some examples of texts that are reviewed are books, films, exhibitions, musical performances and dramatic presentations of all types; they can be reviewed in newspapers, magazines and other media.

Structure: A literary review can contain information about the author/composer or the actors/performers, the characters and the setting where the action takes place. This can be called the **context**. This is followed by a summary of the incidents (**text description**). Finally, the reviewer makes an **evaluative response** (judgment), which indicates what he/she thinks of the text and its appeal to the assumed audience.

A preliminary stage to a literary review is a **personal response**, in which students give spoken responses to a literary text, a film, a piece of art, a building—anything that involves creative composition.

Grammatical features:

- relating, action, saying and thinking verbs used with noun groups to describe characters
- the use of the present tense (which may change to the past tense if the text has a historical setting)
- a time sequence of events, because only the key events are summarised
- the use of pervasive language when the author is making a judgment
- clause or sentence themes that are often the title of the book or the title of other creative pieces of composition
- the name of the author, actors, directors or performers.

These choices clearly locate the reader in a response text.

A review of *Storm Boy*

Genres or text types

Structure	Text	Some language features
Context	*Storm Boy* **is** a novel by the Australian author Colin Thiele. It **is** an exciting story about the friendship between a boy and a pelican that the boy raised from a chick.	relating verbs in the present tense
Text description	Storm Boy **lives** with his father, Hide-Away Tom, in a humpy in a wild part of South Australia beside the Southern Ocean. The area is also a sanctuary for many species of birds. Storm Boy and his father live an isolated life collecting "treasures" blown in with the tide, and befriending all living creatures. He is a happy boy who **loves** the wild storms that lash the area.	timeless present tense sensing (feeling/thinking) verb
	Storm Boy raises the pelican, [**which he calls Mr Percival**], [**when hunters kill the bird's parents and destroy the nest**]. After rescuing and raising Mr Percival, Storm Boy **tries** to return him to the bird sanctuary, but the pelican keeps on coming back. They become best friends and spend every day with each other. Boy and bird have many adventures but eventually Mr Percival **is killed** by hunters **who are illegally hunting in the sanctuary**. This changes Storm Boy's life forever.	adjectival clause adverbial clause action verbs in the present tense passive voice adjectival clause
Judgment	I really **enjoyed** the book, particularly the descriptions of Ninety Mile Beach and the animals that live there. The words paint	sensing (feeling) verb

65

pictures in your mind. [It is an easy book to read because it is not very long and the interesting story makes you want to read to find out what happens next].
— *adverbial*
— *complex sentences*

The ending is a little bit sad but it is also a hopeful ending.
— *compound sentence*

I would recommend this book for primary school boys and girls.

Poetry

Social purpose: Poetry is written to achieve a wide range of social purposes. Poetry expresses feelings and reflections on experience, people and events. It is primarily an aesthetic experience that works mainly through emotions, sensory experience and imaginative perceptions. It may concentrate on the feelings and reflections of the poet or it may tell a story. It describes people, places or things in poetic ways that makes it distinguishable from prose, especially by creating images in striking ways through techniques such as simile, metaphor, alliteration, assonance and onomatopoeia. Sound qualities in the form of rhyme and rhythm are an important component of poetry. However, the main purpose of poetry is to give enjoyment through an understanding of the many literary and language devices that are part of poetry and that are used to concentrate and enhance meaning.

Structure: Poetry is often written in 'chunks' or stanzas. The form that a stanza takes may involve a predetermined structure like the ode or haiku, or it may be free-formed and have meaning dictating the length of each line rather than a prescribed pattern of rhyme and rhythm. Literary devices are used to enhance meaning, and words are used that compress meaning so that poetry is the best possible words used in their best possible order.

There are many recognised types or forms of poems. Here are some, listed in alphabetical order: acrostic poem, ballad, catalogue poem, cinquain, concrete poem, diamante, Dylan Thomas portrait, epic, Ezra Pound couplet, free verse, haiku, limerick, lyric, ode, sonnet.

Grammatical features: These vary enormously depending on the social purpose of the poem but most rely on features of textural cohesion such as word chains based on devices like repetition, synonym and antonym. Story poems use features of story texts such as action verbs, noun groups, adverbials and adverbial clauses, and adjectivals.

Sort of brown

Most things aren't any real colour — *being verb*

in my town; — *rhyme*

[they're sort of brown,] — *figurative language (simile)*

like dust and dead leaves — *figurative language (alliteration)*

and sleeves — *rhyme*

that had been on people — *repetition (cohesion)*

for a day or two.

Most things aren't red or green — *word chain (cohesion)*

or yellow or blue; — *rhyme*

[they're sort of brown]

I think. — *thinking verb*

Don't you?

(Gordon Winch)

🍎 Factual texts

Factual description

Social purpose: Factual description focuses our attention on the characteristic features of a particular thing. It may relate to a person and may contain some personal comment by the author; it may be an interpretative impression of a particular event; or it may be a description that depends on the scrupulous and meticulous detailing of time and events.

Structure: A factual description is made up of an introduction to the subject being described, followed by a description of the characteristic features of that subject, and may conclude with a comment by the author. It has the same structure as a literary description but differs from it because the resulting factual description is based on direct observation rather than on the observation and description made by someone else.

The common grammatical features are the same as those involved in ***literary description*** *(see pp. 61–4)*.

Functional grammar

Information report

Social purpose: An information report gives factual information about a class of things, such as **oceans**, **sharks**, **cats** or **parents**.

Structure: An information report is made up of a general statement about the subject including information that may define and classify that subject, followed by a description that may contain comment about its importance. *(See also Factual description p. 67)*

Grammatical features:

- the use of general nouns
- the use of relating verbs to describe features
- the use of action verbs to describe behaviour
- the use of the timeless present tense of verbs to indicate usualness
- the use of technical terms
- the use of paragraphs with a topic sentence that organises bundles of information
- repeated naming of the topic or generalised subject of the text as the beginning focus of the clause.

Sharks

Structure	Text	Some language features
General statement about a class of things	Sharks are among the largest, deadliest and most feared creatures in the sea. Yet most are harmless and many make excellent eating.	relating verbs general noun cohesive tie
Facts	Sharks have been in the oceans for 350 million years. They are survivors because they are bold and active animals. There are at least 350 different species of sharks that can be divided into two groups; the sharks with cigar-shaped bodies and the rays which have flattened bodies.	relating verb adjectival phrase adjectival (clause)

68

Facts	Sharks and rays have no bones. Their	— timeless present tense
	skeletons [**are made**] from **cartilage**. You	— technical nouns
	can feel cartilage at the tip of your nose or	
	the top of your ears.	
Facts	Sharks have their mouths below their	
	snouts. **Also, they** have five to seven gill	— cohesive tie
	slits on either side of their heads. Fish only	
	have one gill on either side.	

Note: Repeated naming of the topic—sharks

Procedure

Social purpose: A procedure tells us how to do or make something. Recipes, rules of games, how to grow things and how to go from place to place are examples of procedures.

Structure: A procedure is made up of a goal for the activity; a list of any skills, equipment and materials needed to achieve that goal; and, finally, the steps or instructions that show you what to do. These may be numbered.

Grammatical features:
- the use of commands
- the use of action verbs in the present tense
- the use of precise vocabulary
- the use of adverbs and adverbial phrases/clauses that express details of time, place and manner.

A **procedural recount** is the retelling or rewriting of a set of procedures that have been formulated by someone else. They may not reflect personal experience. Telling how a famous chef cooks a particular dish can be a procedural recount.

Functional grammar

How to make a chocolate milkshake

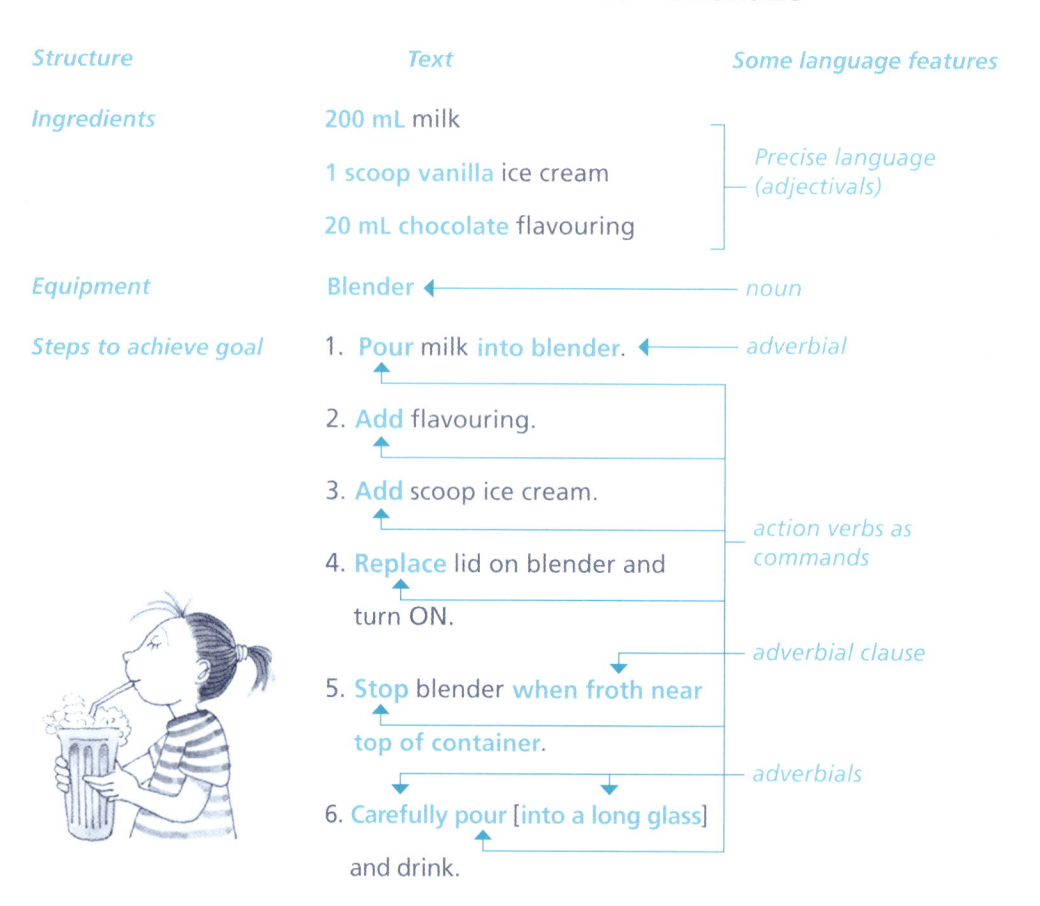

Structure	Text	Some language features
Ingredients	200 mL milk 1 scoop vanilla ice cream 20 mL chocolate flavouring	*Precise language (adjectivals)*
Equipment	Blender	*noun*
Steps to achieve goal	1. Pour milk into blender.	*adverbial*
	2. Add flavouring.	
	3. Add scoop ice cream.	*action verbs as commands*
	4. Replace lid on blender and turn ON.	
	5. Stop blender when froth near top of container.	*adverbial clause*
	6. Carefully pour [into a long glass] and drink.	*adverbials*

Note: Some articles and prepositions are omitted from the text.

Factual recount

Social purpose: A structural recount documents a series of events and attempts to evaluate their significance in some way. Accounts of holidays, school visits and sporting events are all factual recounts. Examples are **Our Mountain Adventure**, **A Trip to the Zoo** and **When We Watched the Grand Final**.

Structure: A factual recount is structured by beginning with an orientation that gives you information about the people and the happenings in the recount (who, when, where and why) followed by a record of events in the order they occurred. Personal comments, which may include making a judgment, are often interspersed throughout the record of events. The text concludes with a reorientation that rounds off the sequence of events.

Grammatical features:

- the use of nouns and pronouns to identify characters or events
- the use of adjectives or adjectival phrases/clauses to describe these subjects

- the use of action verbs to refer to events
- the use of past tense verbs to locate events in relation to the speaker's or writer's time
- the use of adverbs or adverbial phrases/clauses to indicate place and time
- the use of conjunctions and connectives to sequence the events.

Our excursion to Manly

Structure	Text	Some language features
Orientation	Last Wednesday, our class went on an excursion to Manly beach.	
Record of events	We left school at about nine o'clock and walked down to the station. We caught the train and got off at Circular Quay. We were just in time for the ferry.	adverbials (phrases) to show time and place / pronouns to signify group
Events	On the trip over to Manly, we had to cross the Heads. Here the sea was very rough and the waves crashed over the bow of the ferry. Some kids were a bit afraid.	relating verb / action verb
Events	We arrived at Manly and walked across to the ocean beach where we had our lunch. Our teacher, Mr Downard, told us many interesting things about Manly and how it got its name.	pronoun to signify group / action verb / saying verb
Events	At about two o'clock we went back to the wharf to catch the ferry for the trip home. It was still rough crossing the Heads.	pronoun to signify group

Note: The beginning of each paragraph gives the sequence of events.

Genres or text types

71

Functional grammar

Explanation

Social purpose: An explanation tells how something works or why it occurs in the way it does. Explanations are usually found in scientific and technical fields. Examples are *How Fish Breathe*, *How Bees Make Peaches*, *Why Storms Occur*, *Why Plants Need Sunlight* and *Why Lightning is Dangerous*.

Structure: An explanation begins with an introduction that states what is to be explained, followed by a series of steps in the explanation. An explanation may conclude with a final statement that sums up. An explanation may include diagrams, illustrations, charts and/or tables.

Grammatical features:

- the use of general and abstract nouns
- the use of noun groups for greater precision
- the use of technical language
- the use of action verbs in the simple present tense
- the use of the passive voice
- the use of adverbs or adverbial phrases/clauses especially using conjunction of time (when) and cause (why)
- the use of compound sentences extending meaning.

How the telephone works

Structure	Text	Some language features
Introduction	A telephone works like the human ear. The vibrations of the speaker's vocal chords produce air vibrations which make the listener's eardrums vibrate. These vibrations are magnified and our hearing nerves carry the sound message to our brain.	noun group — *The vibrations of the speaker's vocal chords* / *vibrations*; technical language (noun) — *vibrations*; technical language (adjective) — *magnified*; abstract noun — *message*
Explanation	Telephones allow this process to take place over distances where speech wouldn't carry.	general noun — *Telephones*; adjectival (clause) — *where speech wouldn't carry*

Explanation   A telephone **has** a **handpiece**. In the **handpiece** there **is** a **transmitter** and a **receiver**. The **transmitter contains** a **diaphragm** that vibrates. When we **speak** into the **mouthpiece**, vibrations are set up and these **strike** the diaphragm. As the diaphragm vibrates, it changes the electric current and these changes are transmitted.

— technical language (nouns)
— relating verbs
— technical language (nouns)
— action verbs in simple present tense

Explanation   The receiver also has a diaphragm that **vibrates** [**because of the current coming into the phone**]. The vibrations in the diaphragm make vibrations in the air and these reach the listener's ear. Consequently, we are able to hear the sound.

— adverbial clause of reason

Exposition

Social purpose: An exposition argues a case for or against a point or view or belief. Its purpose is to argue a case and to persuade someone to agree with the argument. Examples are *We Should Save Water*, *We Should Save the Trees* and *We Should Ride Bikes*.

Structure: An exposition is made up of an opening statement that describes the position taken. This is followed by a statement supporting that position. This statement must be supported with evidence. The first statement made is usually the strongest argument supported with the most compelling evidence. The following arguments may not be as easily defended because of the available evidence. The order in which 'point and elaboration' are arranged depends on the author. Finally, there will be a concluding statement that restates the opening position more forcefully in the light of the evidence presented.

Grammatical features:

- the use of general and abstract nouns and will probably contain technical words
- the use of evaluative adjectives that give weight to the nouns and reinforce the author's commitment to the argument

- the use of relating, action and thinking verbs
- the use of modal verbs and adverbs to reinforce the author's commitment to a position
- the use of connectives to give order and structure to the evidence-supported position.

The most common form of oral exposition is the **debate**, where teams argue for or against a stated position. It is the role of the affirmative side to make the case for the given proposition. This must be supported by evidence. The negative side presents evidence that contradicts the evidence presented by the other side. There are three speakers for each side. The first speaker introduces the argument and makes points and elaborates through evidence. This strategy is reinforced by the second speaker. Speakers on the other side argue against the propositions and present new evidence or refute the stated evidence. It is the role of the last speaker to sum up with telling points that restate the team's position forcefully and refute the position and evidence presented by the other side. The adjudicator makes a judgment about which side is more convincing.

Ban cars from our cities

Structure	Text	Some language features
Introduction	Cars **should** be banned from our major cities. Our cities **are** heavily polluted and cars are one of the main causes of this. Cars **are** also **dangerous** and **noisy**.	modal verb / relating verbs / adjectivals (evaluative)
Argument	Cars contribute a lot to the pollution of our cities. Cars' exhaust gases are deadly to humans. These gases cause lung diseases like **asthma** and **bronchitis**. Many people end up in hospital because of these **diseases**.	technical nouns / general noun
Argument	**Secondly**, many people live and work in our cities. Cities are busy places with pedestrians clogging narrow footpaths or rushing across busy streets. Cars make such crossings very dangerous. **Pedestrians**	connective / general noun

          are **knocked** over and sometimes **killed** by — *action verbs*
          careless motorists. Everyone **knows** that — *sensing (thinking) verb*
          cars are the biggest killers on our roads.

Argument   **Lastly**, cars are very noisy. During the day — *connective*
          this noise distracts workers. Noise can also
          make telephone conversations **difficult**. — *adjectival*
          At night city residents find it very hard
          to sleep **because of the traffic noise**. — *adverbial (phrase)*
          Sometimes when you are at the pictures
          you can hear the traffic noise. This **can**
          spoil your enjoyment of the movie. — *modal verbs*

Concluding   Our cities **would be** healthier, **much** safer
statement   and **less** noisy places if cars were banned
reinforcing   from the streets. — *modal adverbs*
position

Discussion

Social purpose: A discussion presents both sides of an argument. It enables us to hear, read and write different points of view about a subject such as **Global Warming**.

Structure: A discussion is made up of a statement that outlines an issue and is often accompanied by some background information about that issue. Arguments for and against the proposition should include supporting evidence. A discussion, which involves weighing up the arguments, should conclude this text. This might sum up both sides of the argument or it may include a recommendation in favour of one side.

Grammatical features:

- the use of general nouns
- the use of detailed noun groups to provide information in a compact way
- the use of relating verbs to provide information about the issue
- the use of thinking verbs to express the author's personal view
- the use of adverbs or adverbial phrases/clauses of manner
- the use of modal adverbs to express degree
- the use of additive, contrastive and causal connectives to link arguments.

Functional grammar

Work and play – which is more important?

Structure	Text	Some language features
Introductory statement	Which is the more important part of our lives – work or play? **Work** is doing something because it will bring a benefit. **Play** is doing something for its own sake because we like doing it. Play is what we do when we are not working or doing things like sleeping, washing ourselves or eating.	— general nouns
Arguments for and against	Most of the **activities** that we do at school are work. Through **schoolwork** we learn many useful things. I **think** reading, writing, maths and all the other subjects are important. They give us skills that we can use throughout our lives. I also **believe** it is important to learn and work hard to gain the **skills** necessary for a good job later in life. We work at home too. We work at home because we are part of a family and work helps both the family and us.	— sensing (thinking) verbs — general nouns
	On the other hand, **imagine** our **lives** if all we did was work. How boring would that be? You **might** have heard this old saying: "All work and no play makes Jack a dull boy."	— modal verb
	Play is anything we do because we enjoy it. It **might** be a game, or going to the	— general noun — modal verb

beach, or seeing a movie, or just visiting a friend or relative. **However**, I believe play can also teach us many things. It can teach us how to work together and be a member of a group. **For example**, playing in a team makes us think of someone other than ourselves. Play **often** involves doing physical things, **so play also has an important part in keeping us fit and well**.

Conclusion **In conclusion**, we need both work and play in our lives. We learn from both and both **can** be enjoyable. **In addition**, both work and play **can** help us to be mentally and physically fit. **The most important thing in life** is to get the balance between work and play just right.

Sometimes this is harder than you think!

connectives
modal adverb
adverbial clause of reason
modal verbs
detailed noun group

🍎 Register/social context

Register refers to the way a particular situation affects the language in a text.

Register will change according to the *topic*. You may feel very strongly about an event or an experience. That heightened feeling will influence the register.

Register will also change according to the *people involved*; you will speak differently to someone you really like.

Register will change according to whether the *language* is spoken or written. Spoken language has many short sentences and few content words; written language has longer sentences and many content words.

These things and others affect the register of a piece of discourse.

Below is an example of two different pieces of language. They are both about the same subject and the same participants are involved. One difference in register comes from the fact that the first piece is spoken by the participants, face to face, and the second piece is a letter written by one driver.

Text 1

The accident

First driver: You ran into the back of me! You hit my car!

Second driver: Why did you stop so suddenly?

First driver: I had to brake; there's a sharp corner.

Second driver: I couldn't stop when you braked like that.

First driver: It's your fault; you were too close. Look at my car! I'm calling the police.

Second driver: Call them then; we'll see who's in the wrong.

First driver: That man over there saw what happened. He can be a witness. He'll back me up. What's your name and address?

Text 2

Dear Sir,

I have decided to report yesterday's accident to my insurance company.

You will be hearing from them in due course.

The detail of the accident has been explained, particularly regarding the fact that you hit my car from behind and were not travelling at a safe distance.

I regret that the matter was not reported to the police immediately, but I have now informed them of the incident together with the name of the witness who saw the accident.

Yours,

_____

🍎 Differences in texts

The following diagram shows how various factors affect differences in a text.

The culture
(Cultural context)

The purpose
(Genre—text type)

The situation
(Register—social context)

The subject matter — **Who is involved** — **The channel of communication**
(Field) (Tenor) (Mode)

THE TEXT

Functional grammar

Subject matter **(Field)**	Who is involved **(Tenor)**	The form of the language **(Mode)**
through	through	through

Participants
Persons, places, things
- Noun group (Nominal)

Mood
Declarative, interrogative, imperative
- Sentences
- Statements
- Questions
- Commands

Theme
(First part of a message)
(Prominent foregrounded)
- Noun group
- Verb group
- Adverb group
- Prepositional phrase

Attributes
(Qualities of participants)
- Noun groups
- Adjectives

Modality
Degree of usuality and probability
Obligation
- Adverb groups
- Modal groups (*must, should*)

Rheme
(Remainder of sentence)

Processes
Doing, being, thinking, saying
- Verb groups

Cohesion
(Links in the message)
- Pronouns
- Conjunctions

Circumstances
How, when, where, why
- Adverb groups
- Prepositional phrases

Nominalisation
- Turning other parts of speech into nouns

Voice of verbs
- Active or passive

EXPERIENTIAL **INTERPERSONAL** **TEXTUAL**

WORD STRUCTURES IN THE TEXT

80

🍎 Clause structures to represent experience

These consist of:		These can be:
Participants	persons, places, things and ideas	nouns noun groups/phrases pronouns adjectivals
Attributes	describe the participants	adjectivals noun groups
Processes	action/doing, being, saying, sensing (thinking/feeling)	verbs verb groups/phrases
Circumstances	things that surround the event; how, when, where, why	adverbials adverbial clauses

Example

At the airport the passengers talked quietly about the flight. They were very excited.

Circumstance	At the airport
Participants	the passengers
Process	talked
Circumstance	about the flight
Participant	They
Process	were
Attribute	very excited

🍎 Language structure of personal interaction

Through sentence types

These consist of:		These can be:
Declarative	statement	mood: indicative
Interrogative	question	mood: interrogative
Imperative	command	mood: imperative

Different grammatical moods are found to be more common in different genres. For example, the instruction on p. 70 contains verbs in the imperative mood.

Through modality

These consist of: **These can be:**

Degrees of usuality   often, sometimes, always, seldom, never   adverbs of time

Degrees of certainty   possibly, probably, maybe   modal adverbs

Degrees of obligation   must, should, ought, will   auxiliary verbs or modals

🍎 Language structures for constructing texts

Theme

The ***theme*** comes first in a clause. It is the predominant part. The pattern of the themes in a text shows how the text develops.

Rheme

Rheme is the remainder of the clause.

Example

Theme	Rheme
At the airport	the passengers talked quietly about the flight.
They	were very excited.

Cohesion

Cohesion links ideas in the text.

At the airport | the passengers | talked quietly about the flight.
They | were very excited.

Types of cohesion

1. Reference: Pronouns that refer back to nouns.
   The man was tall and he was thin.

2. Substitution: Using a different word.
   My dog is a good one.

3 Ellipsis: Leaving out words.

The man was tall and (he was) thin.

4 Conjunction: Phrases, clauses, sentences and paragraphs can be linked with conjunctions or adverbs.

The captain and the crew came on shore.

He ran hard; then he swerved.

5 Related words

The man was a thief, a criminal, a villain.

🍎 Sentences in functional grammar

Simple, compound and complex

See **Sentences** pp. 47–51.

Group/phrase structures in functional grammar

Noun group/phrase

This is a group of words built around a head word that is a noun. It often contains articles and adjectives. It is also referred to as the nominal group.

a big, ripe, red apple

*(See **Nouns** pp. 1–6, **Adjectives** pp. 15–19 and **Articles** p. 36)*

Verb group/phrase

This is a group of words built around a head word that is a verb.

might have been stolen

*(See **Verbs** pp. 19–28 and **Compound and auxiliary verbs** pp. 26)*

Adverb group/phrase

This is a group of words built around an adverb.

very quickly

*(See **Adjectives** p. 15 and **Adverbs** p. 29)*

Adjective group/phrase

This is a group of words built around an adjective.

very beautiful

*(See **Adjectives** pp. 15–19)*

Functional grammar

🍎 More about verbs *(See also Verbs pp. 19–29)*

In functional grammar verbs are called *processes*.

There are many kinds of processes. They are:

- action (doing)   (material process)
- saying   (verbal process)
- sensing (thinking/feeling) (mental process)
- timeless present (being) (existing process)
- relational (linking)   (joining or relational process)

The water **rippled** in the light wind. — *action*

It **seemed** ghostly in the moonlight. — *relational*

"Do you **think** anyone **is** here?" John — *relational (linking)* / *sensing (thinking)*

whispered. — *saying*

Simon **imagined** all kinds of terrifying possibilities as he **turned** to his friend, and in an unconvincing voice, **said**, "Not a chance, Johnny, not a chance." — *sensing (thinking)* / *action (doing)* / *saying*

🍎 More about nouns *(See Nouns pp. 1–6)*

In functional grammar, nouns or noun groups are called *participants*. Participants can be persons, places, things or ideas. Persons are human participants; others are non-human participants.

Noun group (Human participant)	Verb group	Noun group (Non-human participant)
The small boy	was eating	a juicy apple.

Noun groups can contain adjectives, articles and other parts of speech.

Traditional/functional terms

Here is a list of some of the words you have met or will meet in this book. They are important in understanding traditional and functional grammar.

Adjective	Main idea	Pronoun
Adverb	Mood	Sentence
Auxiliary verb	Mood, subjunctive	Subject and predicate
Clause	Noun	Subordinate clause
Cohesion	Participle	Tense
Conjunction	Phrase	Verb
Finite verb	Preposition	Voice
Inflection	Principal clause	

This chart will help you see how some traditional and functional grammar terms relate to one another.

It will be very useful when you are learning about functional grammar.

Terms in traditional grammar	Terms in functional grammar	What they mean
Adjective or adjectival phrase	Attribute or adjectival	A word or phrase that adds meaning to a noun
Adverb or adverbial phrase	Circumstance or adverbial	A word or phrase that adds meaning to a verb, adjective or other adverb
Auxiliary verb	Auxiliary verb	A part of a verb that makes up the verb group. It shows tense or mood
Clause	Clause	A group of words with a finite verb
Conjunction	Conjunction	The linking of ideas in a text
Connections between different parts of speech, sentences and paragraphs (cohesion)	Cohesion Reference Substitution Ellipsis Conjunction Lexical (related words)	A joining word in a text
Finite verb	Finite verb	A verb that has a subject

85

Functional grammar

Terms in traditional grammar	Terms in functional grammar	What they mean
Inflection	Inflection	A suffix added to a noun or verb to show number or tense
Main idea at beginning of clause	Theme and rheme	The placing of the main idea (theme) at the beginning of a clause for emphasis. The rheme is the remainder of the clause
Mood Indicative Imperative	Mood and modality Declarative Interrogative Imperative	Verb forms that indicate statements, questions and commands
Mood Subjunctive	Modality	Doubts, wishes, possibility, probability or certainty expressed through modal auxiliary (traditional) or modals and modifiers (functional)
Noun	Participant Also represented by pronouns and noun groups	The name of a person, place or thing
Participle	Participle	Part of a verb in a verb group (or verb phrase) or used as an adjective
Phrase	Phrase	A group of words without a finite verb doing the work of different parts of speech
Preposition	Preposition	A word that introduces a prepositional phrase
Principal clause	Independent clause	A clause that has a single, self-contained message; it can stand by itself
Pronoun	Participant	A word that stands instead of a noun. In functional grammar, pronouns can constitute the noun group
Sentence	Sentence Clause complex	One or more clauses linked together in meaning. One clause must be the principal (or independent) clause. Each sentence begins with a capital letter and ends with a full stop, question mark or exclamation mark
Subject and predicate	Participant and process with an optional circumstance	The subject is the focus of the verb. The predicate contains the finite verb and its modifiers

Terms in traditional grammar	Terms in functional grammar	What they mean
Subordinate clause	Dependent clause Embedded clause	A clause that is linked to a principal clause A subordinate clause cannot stand alone
Tense Present Past Future	Tense Present and timeless present Past Future	The form of the verb that indicates when the action occurs
Verb	Process (Also shown by verb groups including modifiers)	A word in a sentence that states what is happening
Voice Active Passive	Voice Active Passive	In the active voice in traditional grammar, the subject is the doer. In the passive voice, the subject is acted upon In functional grammar, the doer is the theme and the receiver of the action is in the theme position

Some additional terms

Adjectivals   These are various types of words that provide information about the noun and may become part of that noun group. They may be articles (*the*), pointing words, which are also known as demonstratives (*this*, *those*), or possessives, (*my*, *our*, *their*, *your*, *John's*). These three categories are known as **determiners**.

Adjectives can express quantity (*two*), opinion (*difficult*), fact (*round*), comparison (*softer*, *more beautiful*, *busiest*, *the worst*), or classification (*Australian*, *mobile [phone]*). More information can be added to the noun with the use of adjectival phrases or adjectival clauses.

> the girl with the blond hair
>
> the old lady who lived in China

Adverbials   These are the words, groups or phrases in a clause that tell how, when, where or why. Adverbials provide extra detail about what is going on. There are two main categories of adverbials: adverbs and adverbial phrases. Adverbials can modify a verb, an adjective or another adverb.

Functional grammar

> The dog barked in a threatening way.
>
> a very red face
>
> too slowly

Adverbials and adverbial clauses are called **circumstances** in functional grammar.

Causality This is the way ideas are linked in a text to show how one thing causes another.

> We like bananas so we had some for lunch.

The links are often shown by conjunctions such as **so** and **because**.

Clause complex When clauses combine they form a clause complex. Any clause complex is a sentence.

Collocation Collocation refers to words that typically go together, like **bread and butter**, **bacon and eggs**, **tall and thin**.

Determiners Determiners are dependent on nouns. They determine things about the noun.

> the apple   a football   some fruit

Determiners are adjectives or articles.

Embedded clause This is a subordinate (dependent) clause within a principal (independent, main) clause. The embedded clause becomes part of the noun group.

> The girl who had long hair won the prize.

Head word This is the main word in a word group. It may be a noun in a noun group (six big **boxes**), an adjective in an adjectival group, a verb in a verb group or an adverb in an adverbial group.

Modality Modality is concerned with degrees of possibility, probability, certainty or obligation. It is expressed through auxiliary verbs or modifiers.

> may be   should go   certainly

Modifier A modifier is an adverb or an adverb group.

Morphology Morphology is concerned with word structure. It is to do with morphemes. **Morphemes** are the roots and affixes of words.

There are two kinds of morphemes:

Free (or unbound). These are words, or parts of words, that can stand on their own.

For example, the word *railway* consists of two free or unbound morphemes, *rail* and *way*.

Bound. These morphemes cannot stand on their own. They must combine with free morphemes.

For example, the word *unhealthy* consists of the prefix **un** and *healthy*.

Bound morphemes include:
- prefixes and suffixes—<u>re</u>build, kind<u>ness</u>
- inflection—beach<u>es</u>
- possession—dad<u>'s</u> coat
- tense markers—jok<u>ing</u>, play<u>ed</u>
- agreement in person and number—it rattle<u>s</u>

Nominalisation This is the process of forming nouns from other parts of speech.

For example:

invade   invasion
lose   loss

Open and closed word classes **Open** word classes are often called *content* words. They can be added to as language grows and changes.

For example:

astronaut, soap, owl, wash, jump, sat, noisy, careful, fantastic, slowly, very, often

Closed word classes are often called *grammatical* words. They cannot be added to.

For example:

he, she, it, we, which, everyone, under, and, or, as, though, if

Restrictive and non-restrictive clauses There is a difference in meaning between these two clauses.

I read his books that I found most interesting.
I read his books, which I found most interesting.

The first sentence, which refers to only some books, contains a restrictive (defining) clause—*that I found most interesting*. This clause is said to be an embedded clause because it refers back to **books**. The clause '*which I found most interesting*' is said to be a non-restrictive or non-defining clause and is preceded by a comma.

Tag questions The tag question is used in speech to give extra confirmation of something that is more or less expected to be true.

You are coming to the beach, aren't you?

The 'aren't you' is the tag so the whole sentence is a tag question.

Timeless present tense A verb is described as being in the timeless present tense if the action is continuous.

John lives here.

WH and yes/no questions WH questions (who, what, where, when, why, how) cannot be answered by Yes or No; Yes/no questions can.

What is your name? (WH question)

Do you like apples? (Yes/No question)

PUNCTUATION

Capital letters

Capital letters are used as the first letter for all proper nouns.

    Brian   London   Pacific Ocean

Titles of special people also take capital letters.

    Captain Smith   Father John   Councillor Yeung

The personal pronoun *I* is always written with a capital letter.

    I   I'd   I'll   I'm   I've

A capital letter is used as the first letter of the first word of every sentence.

    My dog's name is Bill. He's a cocker spaniel.

The main words in the title of a book, a play, a film, a television show and many headings start with capital letters.

    The Adventures of Robin Hood

    The Nargun and the Stars

    Wide World of Sport

    The Einstein Factor

When writing direct speech, a capital letter is used at the beginning of the first word in quotation marks.

    'It's heavy,' said Grandma.

    Robin asked, 'How do you get there?'

However, if a sentence is broken up by the words used to explain direct speech, the second part of that sentence does not take a capital letter.

    'It's good,' said Joan, 'to come back home after a holiday.'

Full stops

At the ends of sentences

A sentence ends with a full stop.

    The cat chased the rat. The rat ran as fast as it could.
    [statement]

    Bring the ball back here.
    [command]

Sentences that report questions end with a full stop. These are called ***indirect questions***.

    'Will you come for a swim?' I asked.
    [direct question]

I asked her if she would come for a swim.
[indirect question]

To indicate abbreviations

Some words are written in a shortened form.

If the first letter and only a part of the word are included, a full stop is used to show there is part of the word missing.

Reverend	Rev.
Major	Maj.
Captain	Capt.
etcetera	etc.
figure	fig.
Crescent	Cres.

Rev. Ng

If the first letter and other letters, as well as the last letter of the word, are included in the abbreviation, *no full stop* is necessary.

Mister	Mr
Doctor	Dr
Father	Fr
Avenue	Ave

If a name that is made up of more than one word is shortened, the first letter of each word is used without full stops in between. (Unimportant words are sometimes left out.) These are called *initialisms*.

United States of America	USA
Western Australia	WA
Australian Capital Territory	ACT
New South Wales	NSW
Eastern Standard Time	EST
Colonial Sugar Refineries	CSR
Member of Parliament	MP
Australian Labor Party	ALP
Liberal Party	LP
Australian Jockey Club	AJC
Royal Prince Alfred Hospital	RPAH
Royal Agricultural Society	RAS

Acronyms (words made up of the first letter of each word forming the name) do not use full stops.

| QANTAS | Queensland and Northern Territory Air Services |
| CSIRO | Commonwealth Scientific and Industrial Research Organisation |

UNICEF   United Nations International Children's Emergency Fund
WHO   World Health Organization

Question marks

An question mark is used at the end of a sentence that is a question.

> Are you coming to school tomorrow?

A question mark is used in direct or reported speech where a question is asked. The question mark is placed straight after the question. A full stop is used at the end of the sentence.

> 'Whose bag is that?' asked the teacher.

A question mark can be used in the middle of a sentence to show the writer is unsure of the information or the spelling contained in that sentence. The question mark shows this uncertainty.

> The race will be held over the long weekend (?) if there are enough starters.
>
> It was a weird (?) film.

Exclamation marks

An exclamation mark is used when the writer wants to show some feeling about the person or event to which he/she is referring. That feeling might be excitement, surprise, anger, disappointment—strong feelings.

> What a surprise!
>
> Yuck!
>
> Thank heavens!
>
> The favourite has fallen!

When an exclamation is included in direct or reported speech, the exclamation mark is placed straight after the exclamation. A full stop is used at the end of the sentence.

> 'What a disaster!' exclaimed the coach.

Some sentences look like questions but are really exclamations. If the speaker requires an answer, then the sentence is a question. But if an answer is not required, the sentence is probably an exclamation.

> Isn't that stupid play!
>
> Will you have a look at that!

Commas

Commas are used in a sentence to give a short pause. Commas make the meaning clearer by separating parts of the sentence.

Commas and lists

Commas are used to separate items in a list.

> Julia had a dog, a cat, a budgie and a goldfish as pets.

In this list, the last pet is *a goldfish*. It is preceded by *and*. In cases such as these, there is no need for a comma.

If the list is very long, a comma before *and* will sometimes make the meaning clearer.

> James had a bike, a scooter, a skateboard, a surfboard, and roller blades.

Commas with adjectives and adverbs

Commas are used when we have two or more adjectives modifying a noun or two or more adverbs modifying a verb.

> Jane is a bright, happy, cheerful student.
> Grant silently, slowly, carefully moved towards the door.

Commas with compound sentences

When two principal clauses are joined by a coordinate conjunction *(and, but, or, nor, for, so, yet)* to form a compound sentence, a comma can be used to separate the clauses. Many writers would not use a comma.

> I was going to come earlier, **but** I had to finish my homework.
> I was going to come earlier **but** I had to finish my homework.

If the two principal clauses are short, there is no need for a comma.

> I missed the train **so** I caught the bus.

Commas with words, phrases and clauses beginning a sentence

Some sentences begin with a connective such as *so* or *however*. Use a comma to separate the connective from the rest of the sentence. The sentence would still have the same meaning if the connective were omitted.

> **However,** I still think you are wrong.

Sentences often begin with a phrase or a clause. A comma is usually placed after the phrase or clause.

> **In the cool of the morning,** we set off to find the old mine.
> **Although Jan was very late,** Edward decided he would wait for her.

Commas separating words, phrases and clauses within sentences

Commas are used to separate words, phrases or clauses that occur within the sentence. These words may add extra information, but they don't change the meaning of the sentence.

I let my budgie, Tom, out of his cage.

Mr Caldwell, our new coach, used to play grade football.

Nicholas, who has just been given a computer game, is bringing it round here to show us.

Commas used in direct speech

With statements

Where the quotation is a statement, a comma is used at the end of the quotation but before the quotation mark (inverted comma). This is followed by the words used to explain direct speech (**said**, **answered**, **replied**, **asked** etc.).

'I'm all right,' I said.

Where a statement is interrupted by the words used to explain direct speech, those words are enclosed by commas.

'I am ready,' he said, 'to do what you ask me to do.'

Because the quoted sentence is a statement, it ends with a full stop, which is placed before the final quotation mark.

With questions and exclamations

Where the quotation is a question or an exclamation, a question mark or an exclamation mark is used at the end of the quotation but before the quotation mark. No comma is needed. This is followed by the words used to explain direct speech. These words end with a full stop.

'Is that you, Tom?' I asked.

'Ouch!' he cried.

Where a question or exclamation is interrupted by the words used to explain direct speech, those words are enclosed by commas, and the question mark or the exclamation mark is used at the end of the quotation but before the quotation mark.

'Do you think,' she asked, 'that I could have a glass of water?'

Quotation, direct speech marks

One use of quotation marks, direct speech marks, is to indicate direct speech. Direct speech is what someone actually says.

'I like juicy apples,' said Mary.

You may use single or double quotation marks.

"I like juicy apples," said Mary.

There are no quotation marks in speech bubbles. The bubbles act as quotation marks; they tell what is actually said.

Quotation marks are needed to show breaks in direct speech.

'I like red apples,' said Mary, 'but I am not fond of green ones.'

If there are quoted words inside a piece of writing in quotation marks, single marks are needed (if you are using double quotation marks).

"I heard them say, 'Is that the person?'," said Jim.

If you are using single quotation marks then double marks are needed for the quoted words.

'I heard them say, "Is that the person?",' said Jim.

Titles of books, poems and other special names require quotation marks around them. If you are using a computer, these special words can go in italics instead.

He read 'The Hobbit'.

I saw the 'Queen Elizabeth' in the harbour.

Our teacher read us 'The Man from Snowy River'.

Quotations require quotation marks.

'A stitch in-time saves nine' is a useful proverb.

'He sent the flintstones flying, but the pony kept his feet' is a line from the poem our teacher read.

🍎 A point to notice

No quotation marks are needed for indirect speech.

Mary said that she liked juicy apples.

Ali yelled that it was his turn to bat.

Apostrophes

An apostrophe is used to show that something has been left out (*contraction*).

can't (cannot)   I'll (I will)   he's (he is)

It is used to show ownership with nouns.

the man's hat

the children's books

the ladies' lunches

A simple rule for the placing of an apostrophe can be used:

When something is owned, place the apostrophe after the last letter of the owner. This rule always works.

the ten athletes' feet

Ask yourself: *Who owns the feet?*

Answer: *The athletes.*

Ask yourself: *What is the last letter of the word* athletes*?*

Answer: *s.*

So the apostrophe goes after the *s* (*athletes'*).

If two or more people share ownership, only the last owner has an apostrophe.
Tim and Mary's house.

If two or more people each own something, each owner has an apostrophe.
Tim's and Mary's noses.

An apostrophe is often used to show the plurals of numbers and letters.
seven s's   four 4's   Mind your p's and q's.

🍎 Points to notice

Some pronouns need apostrophes.
one's foot   another's feet

Possessive pronouns ending in *s* do *not* have an apostrophe.
his   hers   its   ours   yours   theirs
This is hers and that is yours.   I saw its furry tail.

It's is not a possessive. It is the contraction of *it is*.

Semicolons

A semicolon is mostly used between two connected or balanced ideas in a sentence.

A semicolon can often be replaced by a full stop, but this does not show the link between the two parts as strongly as a semicolon.
I do like swimming; it's such fun.
Don't go near the lions; they could eat you up.

Semicolons can be used with connecting words like **however**, **moreover**, **nevertheless**, **then** and **therefore**.
The two dogs are of the same breed; however, they have different personalities.
First we went to the theatre; then we visited the art gallery.

Use a semicolon when you want to separate a list of long items.
I saw the film about wildlife in America; the one about the Sahara Desert; and that one with all the snakes and lizards in it.

🍎 Points to notice

The semicolon is often described as a stop between a comma and a full stop. Do not use the semicolon to join a principal clause to a clause or phrase.

Incorrect   He gave me the sandwich; although I didn't want it.

In this sentence, a comma or no punctuation should be used. Use a comma after a phrase or clause *(see p.93)*.

    Correct   He gave me the sandwich, although I didn't want it.

Semicolons are often used at the ends of lines of poetry.

    One, two,

    Buckle my shoe;

    Three, four,

    Knock at the door;

    Five, six,

    Pick up sticks;

    Seven, eight,

    Lay them straight;

    Nine, ten,

    A good fat hen.

A semicolon can be used when a comma is confusing.

    The words can be used in paragraphs, sentences or phrases; or by themselves.

Colons

A colon introduces more information. The information can be a list, words, phrases or clauses; or a quotation.

    The following clothes should be taken on the trip: a warm jacket, a pullover, three pairs of socks, a pair of jeans, a change of underwear and a strong pair of shoes.

    Buy these things: a packet of peanuts, two loaves of bread and a kilogram of steak.

    The warning read: 'Give up hope all ye who enter here.'

Brackets

Brackets (parentheses) are always used in pairs. They enclose extra information in the form of an example, a comment or an explanation.

    Buy a kilogram of fish (bream) and . . .

    Carlos (a friend of mine) was there.

    Tennis (a game played on a court) is very good exercise.

Dashes

Dashes are like brackets; they enclose extra information. However, they do not have to be in pairs.

    Have an orange—or would you prefer a peach?

Dashes and brackets are used to show sudden changes in thought.

    I have this friend—oops, there's the bell—who's in Year Six.

A dash can be used to show that something being said has been broken off.

    I really would like—

Hyphens

A hyphen links two or more words or word parts that have to do the job of one.

    reddish-brown coat   ten-year-old girl   self-control

They should not be confused with dashes.

The following are some examples of the uses of hyphens:

- with a prefix when the main word starts with a capital letter

    un-Australian   non-English

- with special prefixes

    self-control   re-enter

- to make the meaning clear

    re-creation [created again]

    recreation [sport]

- with fractions and whole numbers

    three-eighths   nine-tenths   twenty-five

- to form compound adjectives (adjectives made up of two or more words)

    greyish-white colour

    half-hearted attempt

    well-known author

- to form some compound nouns.

    brother-in-law   jack-of-all-trades

Always consult your dictionary to check the use of hyphens in words if you are not sure.

Ellipses

The points of ellipsis (…) mark that something has been left out.

    There were many arguments … and this final one …

You can use the points of ellipsis when you are writing a play or a story.

    'I wish …' he said.

CORRECT USAGE

🍎 Confused words

Here is a list of words that are often confused. They are arranged in alphabetical order for easy reference.

If you look for a word and cannot find it, look for the other word with which it is often confused. For example, if you look up **uninterested** you will not find it there. The word it is often confused with is **disinterested**. When you look under '**d**' you will find the word pair **disinterested—uninterested** so this is where you will find **uninterested**.

The entry will tell you about the words and why they are different. Using the correct word helps you communicate your meaning more clearly.

accept   except

accept   A verb meaning 'to receive something'.
They **accept** small gifts from his church.

except   A subordinate conjunction or preposition meaning 'not including'. Links clauses or phrases.
He would have won **except** he pulled a muscle.
They all went **except** me.

acute   chronic

acute   An adjective meaning 'occurring suddenly, lasting only a short time but severe during that time'.
Mum had an **acute** vomiting attack.

chronic   An adjective meaning 'occurring over a long time'.
He has a **chronic** ear problem.

AD   BC

AD   The abbreviation of *Anno Domini*, in the year of our Lord. It refers to the years after the birth of Christ.
Captain Cook came to Australia in **AD** 1770.

BC   The abbreviation of 'before Christ'. It refers to any years before AD 1.
The Romans came to Britain in 55 **BC**.

advice   advise

advice   A noun
I was given good **advice** by my teacher.

advise   A verb
I **advise** you to use your dictionary.

affect effect

affect A verb meaning 'to change'.
I hope the change will not **affect** you too much.

effect A noun—the result of something happening.
The win had a great **effect** on the team.

all ready already

all ready A phrase meaning 'prepared'.
When we were **all ready**, we jumped in the car.

already An adverb meaning 'earlier' or 'beforehand'.
I have **already** told you I won't go to the game.

a.m. p.m.

a.m. An abbreviated form of *ante meridiem* meaning 'the time from midnight to noon'.
We have breakfast at 8 **a.m.**

p.m. An abbreviated form of *post meridiem* meaning 'the time from noon to midnight'.
Afternoon tea is served at 3 **p.m.**

among between

among A preposition used when talking about more than two people or things.
The teacher divided the tennis balls **among** members of her class.

between A preposition that refers to two people or things.
The teacher divided the cake **between** herself and her friend, John.

ante- anti-

ante- A prefix meaning 'before'.
My sister is going to an **ante**natal clinic at the hospital.

anti- A prefix meaning 'against' or 'opposed to'.
My dad took part in the **anti**-war demonstrations.

anxious eager

anxious An adjective meaning 'to be nervous'.
She was very **anxious** waiting for the train to arrive.

eager An adjective meaning 'to look forward to'.
She was **eager** to do well in her exams.

anybody anyone

anybody, anyone, everybody, everyone, nobody, no-one, somebody, someone

Singular pronouns that take a singular verb.
Anybody knows that six and four is ten.

anything anythink

anything   A pronoun meaning 'any thing'.
Anything can happen in this match.

anythink   A non-word that should never be used.

as like

as   A subordinate conjunction that can begin a clause.
I reached for the handle **as** the light went out.

like   A preposition that can begin a phrase.
He plays football **like** his skilful brothers.

assure ensure insure

assure   A verb meaning 'to make confident'.
I **assure** you that your dog will be well cared for.

ensure   A verb meaning 'to make something happen'.
Will you **ensure** that you will be here tomorrow?

insure   A verb meaning 'to buy insurance'.
We will **insure** our house for $200,000.

astrology astronomy

astrology   A noun—study of the supposed effects of the planets and stars on the lives of humans.
Madam Startreck used **astrology** to tell me that next Friday would be an exciting day for me.

astronomy   A noun—study of the universe.
A telescope helps us in our study of **astronomy**.

aural oral

aural   An adjective concerning the ear and hearing.
Her **aural** test proved she needed a hearing aid.

oral   An adjective concerning the mouth and talking.
The **oral** test was harder than the written examination.

bath bathe

bath   A noun—a place where we wash our bodies.
There is a **bath**, a shower and a toilet in the bathroom.

bath   A noun—the act of washing using a bath.
I'm going to have a **bath** before tea.

bath   A verb—an action meaning 'to wash with water'.
I **bath** the baby in a plastic tub.

bathe	A verb meaning 'to clean something with water'. Tom's dad **bathed** his grazed leg.
bathe	A verb that can mean *to swim*. The family **bathed** at Noosa Beach.

began begun

began	The past tense of the verb *to begin*. He **began** swimming when he was five.
begun	The past participle of the verb *to begin*. He has **begun** lessons with a new coach

beside besides

beside	A preposition They sat **beside** the lake.
besides	A preposition meaning 'apart from'. No-one else will be there **besides** John.

biannual biennial

biannual	An adjective describing something that happens twice a year. The group had its **biannual** meetings in April and September.
biennial	An adjective describing something that occurs every two years. The next **biennial** meeting will be held in two years.

both each

both	Means 'two' and always takes a plural verb. **Both** Jim and Jane **are** coming.
each	Means 'one' and always takes a singular verb. **Each has** a good chance of winning the race.

bought brought

bought	The past tense and past participle of the verb *to buy*. We **bought** a new jumper for my young brother.
brought	The past tense and past participle of the verb *to bring*. We **brought** our new baby brother home.

breath breathe

breath	A noun—air going in or out of the lungs. He took a deep **breath** before the dive.
breathe	A verb meaning 'to make air go in or out of the lungs'. He was unable to **breathe** properly during an asthma attack.

broke　broken

broke　The past tense of the verb *to break*.
He **broke** the record last Wednesday.

broken　The past participle of the verb *to break*.
He has **broken** seven records this year.

came　come

came　The past tense of the verb *to come*.
John **came** home at seven o'clock.

come　The past participle of the verb *to come*.
John has **come** home.

can　may

can　A helping verb meaning 'able to do something'.
I **can** climb that tall tree.

can　A noun—a metal container.
I have a **can** of tuna in my pack.

may　A helping verb meaning 'allowed to do something' or 'that you might do something but it isn't certain'.
May I come to your birthday party?

May　A noun—fifth month of the year.
My birthday is in **May**.

cardinal numbers　ordinal numbers

cardinal numbers　A compound noun meaning any ordinary numbers.
There are **30** children in my class.

ordinal numbers　A compound noun that shows place in a series.
Friday will be the **21st** of the month.

cloth　clothe

cloth　A noun—a piece of woven material.
The suit was made from woollen **cloth**.

clothe　A verb meaning 'to put on clothes'.
For the play, I will **clothe** her in old rags.

compare　contrast

compare　A verb used for things that are alike.
Compare this apple to this pear.

contrast　A verb used for things that do not share common qualities.
The blue walls **contrast** with that bright yellow wall.

complement compliment

complement A verb meaning 'to make something complete'.
The rice will **complement** your food supply.

compliment A verb or noun meaning 'to praise someone or something'.
I want to **compliment** your team on its performance.

compliment A noun—a spoken or written expression of praise.
John paid June a **compliment** when he spoke at the function.

continual continuous

continual An adjective describing something that happens again and again over a period of time.
The team's **continual** complaints drove the coach mad.

continuous An adjective describing something that goes on without a break.
The **continuous** noise from the rock band kept me awake.

could have could of

could have A verb phrase
✓ James **could have** been the school captain this year.
✗ James ~~could of~~ been the school captain this year.

could of is used mistakenly because of the confusion of the contraction of *have* ('ve) with *of*. The same applies to *should have* and *would have*.

dairy diary

dairy A noun or adjective—a place where cows are milked.
Mr Holloway used to own a **dairy** at Berry.
His **dairy** cows were all Illawarra Shorthorns.

diary A noun or adjective—a book with a day-to-day record of events.
I keep my **diary** in a secret place.
He makes a **diary** entry for every telephone call.

device devise

device A noun—a tool or simple machine.
Penny invented a **device** for sharpening pencils.

devise A verb meaning 'to make, invent or work out'.
Bruce will probably **devise** a plan for staying away from school.

did done

did The past tense of the verb *to do*.
He **did** his homework every night.

done	The past participle of the verb *to do*.
	He has **done** all his homework so he can watch TV.

different from/than/to

different from	This is the accepted written form of this expression, although modern usage now accepts 'different to'.
	My watch is **different from** my teacher's.
different than	This is not used in written language.
different to	✓ He is **different from** me.
	✗ He is ~~different to~~ me.
	✗ He is ~~different than~~ me.

disinterested uninterested

disinterested	An adjective meaning 'impartial or unbiased'.
	He was a **disinterested** observer at the conference.
uninterested	An adjective meaning 'not interested'.
	William is very **uninterested** in biology.

drove driven

drove	The past tense of the verb *to drive*.
	He **drove** his father's car too fast.
driven	The past participle of the verb *to drive*.
	He has **driven** from Brisbane today.

either … or   neither … nor

either	This is always linked with 'or' and takes a singular verb.
	Either Jim **or** Pete **has** won the race.
neither	This is always linked with 'nor' and takes a singular verb.
	Neither the team **nor** its coach **was** happy.

elder/eldest   older/oldest

elder/eldest	Adjectives describing age relationships within a family.
	John is the **elder** brother.
	Phillip is the **eldest** child in that family.
older/oldest	Adjectives meaning 'more old' or 'most old'.
	That elephant is **older** than its keeper.
	That horse is the **oldest** one in the stable.

emigrate   immigrate

emigrate	A verb meaning 'to move away from the country of your birth'.
	Many people decided to **emigrate** from Italy after the war.
immigrate	A verb meaning 'to arrive and live in a new country'.
	Many Italian, Greek and Turkish families **immigrated** to Australia.

employee employer

employee A noun—the person who is employed.
  James White is an **employee** of the Commonwealth Bank.

employer A noun—a person or company who employs another person.
  The Commonwealth Bank is a very large **employer** in Australia.

everybody nobody somebody

Pronouns used in relation to a group of persons; they take a singular verb.

everybody **Everybody has** a chance to win.
nobody **Nobody is** available to play.
somebody **Somebody is** responsible.
  Modern usage now allows us to use the plural pronoun 'they' with these pronouns.
  Everybody says that **they** should be at school.

everyone no-one someone

Pronouns used in relation to individual persons who make up a group; they take a singular verb.

everyone **Everyone is** guilty.
no-one **No-one is** free to go.
someone **Someone has** to pay.

everything nothing something

Pronouns used in relation to things; they take a singular verb.

everything **Everything is** provided.
nothing **Nothing is** given away.
something **Something is** happening.

explicit implicit

explicit An adjective meaning 'clearly defined, stated or set down'.
  He gave an **explicit** recount of the events.

implicit An adjective meaning 'not clearly defined or stated but implied or suggested'.
  The team has an **implicit** understanding of how the game should be played.

export import

export A verb meaning 'to send out'.
  Australia would like to **export** more uranium.

export A noun
  Our largest **export** is coal.

import A verb meaning 'to bring in'.
  Australia **imports** many foreign-made cars.

import   A noun

Our largest **import** is probably foreign cars.

farther   further

Either is correct; *further* is generally preferred.
The **further** they went, the **further** he dropped behind.
The superlative of *further* is *furthest*.

few   couple

few   An adjective meaning 'more than two things'.

John played a **few** games of football.

couple   An adjective meaning 'two things'.

I had a **couple** of slices of toast for breakfast.

fewer   less

fewer   An adjective that refers to things that can be counted.

There are **fewer** boys than girls in our class.

less   An adjective that refers to something that can't be counted but can be measured.

There is **less** water in the dam than there was last year.

final   finale

final   A noun—the last of a series.

Our team made the **final** last year.

final   An adjective

Is that your **final** offer?

finale   A noun—the last part of a performance.

The orchestra played the **finale** with great style.

flaunt   flout

flaunt   A verb meaning 'to put something on show to make others envious'.

I bet she will **flaunt** her new gown at the B&S Ball.

flout   A verb meaning 'to ignore a rule on purpose'.

Oliver has been known to **flout** the school rules.

formally   formerly

formally   An adverb derived from *formal* meaning 'to do something in a formal way'.

He dressed **formally** for the event.

formerly   An adverb derived from *former* meaning 'something done before'.

He was **formerly** a teacher but now is a writer.

Confused words

former latter

These are pronouns when they work together and refer to people, places and things that have already been mentioned. *Former* is the first of two and *latter* is the last of two.

former Bach and Chopin are famous composers; the **former** was
latter German and the **latter** Polish.

former An adjective meaning 'previously'.
He was the **former** ambassador to Thailand.

from off

from A preposition
I bought it **from** that shop.

off An adverb
The wheels fell **off**.

From and *off* are often confused when writing about exchanging things.
You buy or take *from* a person.
✅ I bought my bike **from** James.
❌ I bought my bike **off** James.

gave given

gave The past tense of the verb *to give*.
He **gave** all his money to charity.

given The past participle of the verb *to give*.
He has **given** her a beautiful book.

gone went

gone The past participle of the verb *to go*.
I had **gone** to the movies.

went The past tense of the verb *to go*.
I **went** to school even though I was sick.

good well

good An adjective
She is a **good** netball player.

good An adverb
The team looked **good**.

well An adverb
They played that match **well**.

There is a difference in meaning between *good* and *well* in these expressions.
Tom is looking **well**. (healthy)

Tom is looking **good**. (doing something well or looking attractive)
Using 'good' in this way is colloquial but now generally accepted.

hanged hung

hanged The past form of the verb *to hang* but refers to a method of execution.

Ned Kelly was **hanged** at Melbourne Gaol.

hung The past form of the verb *to hang* but refers to something rather than someone.

They **hung** the meat in the coolroom.

have of

Have and *of* are sometimes confused because *have* is contracted to *-ve* in such phrases as *could have* (could've), *should have* (should've) and *would have* (would've). *Have* is always a verb. *Of* is a preposition and never a verb.

✓ The team should **have** won that match.
✗ The team should **of** won that match.

he him

he A personal pronoun, third person, nominative case.
He hit the ball over the fence.

him A personal pronoun, third person, objective case.
She hit **him** with the broom.

Other personal pronouns are:
Nominative case: *I, you, he, she, it, we, you, they*
Objective case: *me, you, him, her, it, us, you, them*

honorary honourable

honorary An adjective describing something done for no pay.
He is the **honorary** treasurer of our club.

honourable An adjective describing a person who does good things.
He is a very kind and **honourable** person.

The term *honourable* is used formally in the title of members of parliament.
The **Honourable** John Howard, MP is the prime minister.

hyper- hypo-

hyper- A prefix meaning 'too much'.
She was a **hyper**active child.

hypo- A prefix meaning 'under' or 'too little'.
He was given an injection with a **hypo**dermic needle.

inter- intra-

inter- A prefix meaning 'between' or 'among'.
The cars crashed at the **inter**section.

intra- A prefix meaning 'within' or 'inside'.
When you fly from Sydney to Wagga, you are travelling on an **intra**state route.

laid lain

laid
: The past form of the verb *to lay*. You always lay something somewhere.

    He **laid** the plates on the table.

lain
: The past form of the verb *to lie*. You lie or rest somewhere with your body.

    After you have **lain** down, you will feel much better.

lay lie

lay
: A verb meaning 'to put down'. It always requires an object. You lay something somewhere.

    He **lay** his hand on the table.

lie
: A verb meaning 'to be or rest in a flat position'.

    Every summer, Mum tells me not to **lie** in the sun.
    Also has the meaning 'to tell an untruth'.
    Do not **lie** to me.

lie
: A noun—the untruth that is told.

    Jessica told me a **lie**, Mummy.

learn teach

learn
: A verb meaning 'to acquire knowledge or information'.

    He will **learn** to play the piano when he is three.

teach
: A verb meaning 'to pass on knowledge or information to instruct others'.

    Will you **teach** me how to make chocolate cake?

lend loan

lend
: A verb meaning 'to give to temporarily'.

    I **lend** money to my friends.

loan
: A noun—money or objects you give to someone temporarily.

    ✅ Don gave me a **loan** of five dollars.
    ❌ Don gave me a ~~lend~~ of five dollars.

lightning lightening

lightning
: A noun—discharge of electricity in the atmosphere.

    The **lightning** flashed and the thunder roared.

lightening
: The present participle of the verb *to lighten*, meaning 'reduce weight of'.

    By throwing out sand, he was **lightening** the weight in the balloon.

loose lose

loose
: An adjective meaning 'not tightened or fixed'.

    The **loose** nut caused the accident.

lose   A verb meaning 'to mislay'.
Did you **lose** your front door key?

a lot   many   much

a lot   An adjective used with amounts of things.
There was **a lot** of water in the boat.

many   An adjective used with objects you can count.
There were **many** chairs in the room.

much   An adjective used with amounts of things.
There was too **much** air in the tyres.

loud   loudly

loud   An adjective describing a high volume of noise.
There was a **loud** bang.

loudly   An adverb never used as an adjective.
- ✓ The band played **loudly**.
- ✗ The band played ~~loud~~.

me   my

me   A personal pronoun, first person, objective case.
He gave the ball to **me**.

my   A possessive or pronominal adjective.
- ✓ It's **my** ball.
- ✗ It's ~~me~~ ball.

of   off

of   A preposition indicating distance or direction:
Wollongong is south **of** Sydney.
contents:
a kilogram **of** potatoes
belongings or possessions:
He is a friend **of** mine.

off   A preposition, adverb or adjective meaning 'away from' or 'no longer a part of'.
He slipped and fell **off** the ladder. [preposition]
The wheels fell **off**. [adverb]
The meat is **off**. [adjective]

persecute   prosecute

persecute   A verb meaning 'to act against a person or group in an unjust, cruel way'.
Jews were **persecuted** during the Second World War.

prosecute   A verb meaning 'to take legal action'.
Mr Jones was **prosecuted** for dumping rubbish in the street.

precede proceed

precede
: A verb meaning 'to go before'.
His fame **preceded** him.

proceed
: A verb meaning 'to go forward'.
He **proceeded** to walk down the street at a brisk pace.

prescribe proscribe

prescribe
: A verb meaning 'to order treatment'.
The doctor **prescribed** antibiotics for the infection.

proscribe
: A verb meaning 'to forbid'.
The judge **proscribed** that the families must not meet.

purposefully purposely

purposefully
: An adverb meaning 'to do something with enthusiasm and determination'.
He **purposefully** worked at the portrait of his friend.

purposely
: An adverb meaning 'to do something intentionally'.
He **purposely** avoided seeing his sister.

raise rise

raise
: A verb meaning 'to lift up'. The past forms are *raised*.
He **raised** the banner above his head.

rise
: A verb meaning 'to get up or go upwards'. The past forms of the verb are *rose* and *risen*.
The balloon **rose** above the earth.

rise
: A noun
John has just had a **rise** in his salary.
John has just had a **raise**.
This is now becoming acceptable usage.

ran run

ran
: The past tense of the verb *to run*.
He **ran** in three races.

run
: The past participle of the verb *to run*.
He has **run** in three races.

run
: A noun
Gordon went for a **run** through the bush.

rang rung

rang
: The past tense of the verb *to ring*.
The bell **rang** at 3.20 p.m.

rung
: The past participle of the verb *to ring*.
The bell has **rung** three times this afternoon.

real   really

real
: An adjective meaning 'genuine'.
He is a **real** friend.

really
: An adverb meaning 'truly'.
✓ The weather was **really** foul.
✗ The weather was **real** foul.

receipt   recipe

receipt
: A noun—a document recording something has been paid for.
I paid the money and was given a **receipt**.

recipe
: A noun—list of ingredients and how to use them.
Here is the **recipe** for a rich chocolate cake.

reserve   reverse

reserve
: A verb meaning 'to keep something for a special purpose'.
He **reserved** his seat on the express train.

reverse
: A verb meaning 'to go backwards'.
She **reversed** the car out into the street.

respectable   respectful

respectable
: An adjective meaning 'to have the respect of others'.
She was a **respectable** lawyer.

respectful
: An adjective meaning 'showing respect for others'.
The whole town was **respectful** of the work Father Smith was doing.

rhyme   rhythm

rhyme
: A noun—words that sound the same, like *boy* and *toy*, rhyme.
Some people prefer verse that **rhymes**.

rhythm
: A noun—the beat of music or verse.
The music had a strong Latin **rhythm**.

ridden   rode

ridden
: The past participle of the verb *to ride*.
Have you ever **ridden** a horse?

rode
: The past tense of the verb *to ride*.
I **rode** a horse in Centennial Park last week.

sang   sung

sang
: The past tense of the verb *to sing*.
She **sang** three songs at the concert.

sung   The past participle of the verb *to sing*.
✅ She has already **sung** four verses.
❌ She has already **sang** four verses.

saw   seen

saw   The past tense of the verb *to see*.
✅ I **saw** the accident.
❌ I **seen** the accident.

seen   The past participle of the verb *to see*.
I have **seen** several accidents at this corner.

sewage   sewerage

sewage   A noun—the waste matter that goes down the sewer.
Raw **sewage** is sometimes allowed to flow into the sea.

sewerage   An adjective that describes the system of sewage removal.
The **sewerage** system in Sydney is very old.

shall   will

shall   An auxiliary verb showing future tense. Used in the first person, or in the second and third person to show emphasis.
I **shall** be going on holidays next Monday.
You **shall** be on time! [emphasis]

will   An auxiliary verb showing future tense. Used in the second and third person, and in the first person to show emphasis.
They **will** be going on holidays next Monday.
I **will** be there. [emphasis]

so   that

so   An adverb used to intensify the meaning and used like 'very'.
✅ I was **so** tired I couldn't stay awake.
❌ I was **that** tired I couldn't stay awake.

that   Never an adverb.

sometime   sometimes

sometime   An adverb describing some indefinite point in time.
Sometime soon we will be going on holidays.

sometimes   An adverb meaning 'on some occasions'.
My English uncle visits us **sometimes**.

When *some time* is part of a phrase, it is written as two words.
I will be at school for **some time** to come.

stalactite   stalagmite

stalactite   A noun—a column of rock formed by dripping water.
A **stalactite** grows down from the roof.

stalagmite   A noun—like a stalactite but grows up from the floor.

(Remember the 't' in *stalactite* stands for 'top' so a stalactite grows down from the top. The 'g' in *stalagmite* stands for 'ground' so a stalagmite grows up from the ground).

There are both **stalactites** and **stalagmites** in the Jenolan Caves.

stole   stolen

stole   The past tense of the verb *to steal*.
The thief **stole** Mum's diamond ring.

stolen   The past participle of the verb *to steal*.
My bike has been **stolen**.

subconscious   unconscious

subconscious   An adjective meaning 'just below conscious level'.
Something in his **subconscious** told him not to do it.

unconscious   An adjective meaning 'not conscious'.
He was knocked **unconscious** by a cricket ball.

sympathy for   sympathy with

sympathy for   This means 'to feel sorry for someone'.
I have great **sympathy for** farmers who are fighting the drought.

sympathy with   This means 'to feel sympathy in common with others'.
I have **sympathy with** the idea of Aboriginal land rights.

that/those   this/these

that/those   Demonstrative pronouns or demonstrative adjectives that refer to things that are not close by.
That boat over there seems out of control.
Those birds are being a nuisance to those picnickers.

this/these   Demonstrative pronouns or demonstrative adjectives that refer to things that are nearby or close to.
This book is very old.
These books are very old.

their   theirs

their   Possessive or pronominal adjective, third person, plural.
It is **their** boat.

theirs   Possessive pronoun, third person, plural.
It is **theirs**.

them   they

them   Personal pronoun, third person, plural, objective case.
I gave **them** away.

they   Personal pronoun, third person, plural, nominative case.
- ✓ **They** are all in one family.
- ✗ ~~Them~~ are all in one family.

them those

them   Personal pronoun, third person, plural, objective case.
I gave flowers to **them**.

those   Demonstrative pronoun or demonstrative adjective.
- ✓ **Those** books belong to the library.
- ✗ ~~Them~~ books belong to the library.

translucent transparent

translucent   An adjective meaning 'lets in light but can't be seen through'.
Coloured window blinds are **translucent**.

transparent   An adjective meaning 'able to be seen through'.
Mum uses **transparent** plastic to wrap my lunch.

try try to

try to   A verb form that is usually followed by an infinitive.
Try to finish your homework before tea.
This is preferred to writing *try and*.
- ✓ **Try to** eat your vegetables.
- ✗ ~~Try and~~ eat your vegetables.

unless without

unless   A subordinate conjunction meaning 'except on the condition that'.
I won't go **unless** you go too.

without   A preposition meaning 'not accompanied by, not using or not having'.
I won't go **without** you.

what which

What and *which* can be used as interrogative pronouns or interrogative adjectives.
Which book is it in? **What** book is it in?
Which can also be a relative pronoun while *what* can never be.
- ✓ This is the book **which** I borrowed from the library.
- ✗ This is the book **~~what~~** I borrowed from the library.

🍎 Homonyms

Homonyms are words like *fare* and *fair*, which sound the same but are spelt differently and have different meanings; or words like *desert* (a dry place) and *desert* (to run away from something), which have the same spelling but sound different and have different meanings.

Homonyms like *fare* and *fair* are also called **homophones** because they sound the same. Homonyms like *desert* and *desert* are also called **homographs** because they look the same. Some homonyms like *bow* (to bend over) and *bow* (the front of a boat) are both homophones and homographs.

The word *homonym* means 'the same name' (*homo*, the same; *nym*, name); the word *homophone* means 'the same sound' (*homo*, the same; *phone*, sound); the word *homograph* means 'the same writing' (*homo*, the same; *graph*, writing). For convenience, we will call them all homonyms.

Below is a useful list of homonyms. It is not exhaustive; there are many more, but these are some of the most common.

allowed aloud

- allowed   The past tense and past participle of the verb *to allow*.
  I **allowed** them to come in.
- aloud   An adverb meaning 'to speak audibly or to cry out'.
  He cried **aloud** with pain.

aren't aunt

- aren't   The contraction of *are not*.
  They **aren't** coming to the picnic.
- aunt   A noun—a female relative, the sister of your mother or father.
  My **aunt** lives in Perth.

band banned

- band   A noun—a company or crowd and often musicians. It also means a strip of material used to bind things together.
  The **band** played 'Waltzing Matilda'.
  The papers were held with a rubber **band**.
- banned   An adjective meaning 'forbidden'.
  He was **banned** from playing for two weeks.
- banned   Past tense of the verb *to ban*.
  They **banned** him for seven matches.

bare bear

bare An adjective meaning 'uncovered'.
I had **bare** feet.

bear A noun—an animal.
A polar **bear** is white.

bear A verb meaning 'to carry, hold up or put up with'.
I will **bear** the weight.
I cannot **bear** the pain.

base bass

base A noun—the bottom part of a thing.
the **base** of the cliff.

base A noun—headquarters.
army **base**

bass A noun—the lowest musical pitch.

be bee

be A verb—to exist.
I will **be** home at eight o'clock.

bee A noun—an insect.
The **bee** buzzed around on the bottlebrush flowers.

bean been

bean A noun—an edible vegetable.
A **bean** is green.

been The past participle of the verb *to be*.
I have **been** to see him.

berry bury

berry A noun—a small fruit.
I ate a red **berry**.

bury A verb meaning 'to cover in the ground'.
My dog likes to **bury** his bone.

berth birth

berth A noun—a place where you sleep in a boat or train; a place where a ship ties up at a dock.

berth A verb meaning 'to tie up at a wharf or dock'.
The ship **berthed** at Dock 14.

birth A noun—the process of being born.
the **birth** of the baby

bight   bite byte

bight   A noun—an indentation in the coastline.
The Great Australian **Bight**

bite   A noun
a big **bite** of pie

bite   A verb
to **bite** a piece of pie

byte   A noun—a unit of information stored by a computer.

blew   blue

blew   The past tense of the verb *to blow*.
I **blew** the trumpet.

blue   An adjective
a **blue** sweater

blue   A noun—the name of the colour.
Blue is my favourite colour.
You can also feel *blue* when you are unhappy.

board   bored

board   A noun—a flat piece of wood; the name of a group of people who are in charge of some activity.
The **board** of the company met monthly.

bored   The past tense of the verb *to bore* meaning 'to make a hole'.
The machine **bored** a hole.
It can also mean 'to make someone lose interest'.
The movie **bored** them.

boarder   border

boarder   A noun—someone who lives at school, or someone who pays to live at a place.

border   A noun—the edge or side of a thing.

border   A verb meaning 'to form the edge of a thing'.
The new property will **border** our place.

bough   bow (they both rhyme with *cow*)

bough   A noun—the limb of a tree.

bow   A noun—to take a bow; also the front of a boat.

bow   A verb meaning 'to bend over'.
The actor will **bow** to the audience.

bow   bow (they both rhyme with *so*)

bow   A noun—a knot with two loops.
I wear a **bow** tie.

Homonyms

119

bow   A noun—a device used to fire an arrow.
a **bow** and arrow

bow   A noun—used to play a violin.

boy   buoy

boy   A noun—a male child.

buoy   A noun—a marker in the water.

buoy   A verb meaning 'to support'.
to **buoy** someone up

brake   break

brake   A noun—something that slows a machine.

brake   A verb
Brake as you come to the corner.

break   A noun—a gap; an attempt to escape; a short rest.

break   A verb meaning 'to fracture something'.
Don't **break** the glass.

bread   bred

bread   A noun—made from flour, water and yeast.
I like eating fresh **bread** and butter.

bred   Past tense of the verb *to breed*.
He **bred** cattle on his farm.

buy   by   bye

buy   A verb meaning 'to purchase something'.

buy   A noun meaning 'something that is bought'.
a good **buy**

by   An adverb
They went **by**.

by   A preposition
by the pool

bye   A noun—a run in cricket when the batsman does not hit the ball; a sports match not played.
We had a **bye**.

caught   court

caught   The past tense of the verb *to catch*.

court   A noun—a place where games are played; where royalty and their helpers live; where legal cases are heard.

court   A verb meaning 'to try to win someone's love or favour'.
The prince will **court** the princess.

cell   sell

cell   A noun—a small room in a prison; a tiny part of all living things; a part of a battery; a computer term.

sell   A verb meaning 'to give a thing to someone in exchange for payment'.
Would you like to **sell** that bike?

cent   sent   scent

cent   A noun—one hundredth of a dollar.

sent   The past tense and past participle of the verb *to send*.
I **sent** you a postcard.
You have **sent** me a postcard.

scent   A noun—a pleasant smell; a perfume.

scent   A verb meaning 'to smell'.
The dogs **scented** the fox.

cereal   serial

cereal   A noun—a grain.

serial   A noun—a film, play or story that continues episode by episode.

check   cheque

check   A verb meaning 'to stop or prevent'; 'to see if something is correct'.
to **check** their progress
Check your answers.

check   A noun—something that stops your progress; a term used in chess.
You are in **check**. [in a game of chess]

check   An adjective
a **check** skirt
a **check** point

cheque   A noun—a written order provided by a bank.
I will pay by **cheque**.

choral   coral

choral   An adjective describing something sung by a choir.
a **choral** performance

coral   A noun—the hard, colourful shapes formed from the skeletons of small sea creatures.
coral reef

chord cord

- chord — A noun—a musical term.
  a C major **chord**

- cord — A noun—something used to tie things together.
  a pyjama **cord**

cite sight site

- cite — A verb—to summons to court; to quote a book or author.
  She was able to **cite** many examples to support her argument.

- sight — A noun—the ability to see.
  My uncle has lost his **sight**.

- site — A noun—a place occupied by a specific subject.
  This block of land is the **site** of my new house.

- site — A verb—to locate, place.
  It is hoped to **site** the house on this level area.

coarse course

- coarse — An adjective meaning 'thick or rough' (coarse fabric); 'rude or offensive' (coarse language).

- course — A noun that has many meanings.
  golf **course**
  soup for the first **course**
  a **course** of lessons
  The ship's **course** was north.

- course — An adverb in the phrase 'of course'.

council counsel

- council — A noun—a group of men and women who make decisions as a group.
  My dad works for the local **council**.

- counsel — A noun—advice given after much careful thought.
  My grandfather gave me wise **counsel**.

- counsel — A verb meaning 'to advise and recommend'.
  Pupils should **counsel** with their teachers.

creak creek

- creak — A noun—a squeaky sound.

- creak — A verb meaning 'to make a squeaky sound'.
  The door **creaked**.

- creek — A noun—a small stream.

currant current

currant   A noun—a dried fruit.

current   A noun—a flow of water, electricity or air.

current   An adjective meaning 'belonging to the present; happening at this moment'.
a **current** issue

days daze

days   A noun—the plural of *day*.
the **days** of the week

daze   A verb meaning 'to stun, confuse or bewilder'.
He was **dazed** by the blow.

daze   A noun.
to be in a **daze**

dear deer

dear   An adjective meaning 'greatly loved'; 'costing too much'; 'respected'.
my **dear** friend
a very **dear** cut of meat
Dear Sir

deer   A noun—an animal.

desert dessert

desert   A noun (with stress on the first syllable—*dés.ert*)—a dry place.

desert   An adjective
desert region

desert   A verb (with stress on the second syllable—*de.sért*) meaning 'to run away from or leave something'.
Do not **desert** your post.

dessert   A noun—sweets at the end of a meal.
We had apple pie for **dessert**.

dew due

dew   A noun—small drops of water on the grass.

due   An adjective meaning 'ready to arrive' or 'expected'.
The train is **due**.

die dye

die   A verb meaning 'to stop living'.

dye   A noun—a substance used to make something another colour.
The **dye** was dark red.

dye   A verb meaning 'change the colour'.
Will you **dye** your old coat?

draw   drawer

draw   A verb meaning 'to make a picture with a pen or pencil'.

draw   A noun—a game that ends with both sides having equal scores.

drawer   A noun—a box that slides in and out of a desk or cupboard.
a chest of **drawers**

ewe   yew   you

ewe   A noun—a female sheep.

yew   A noun—a type of tree.

you   A pronoun, second person singular or plural personal.
You are my friend.

fair   fare

fair   An adjective meaning 'light in colour'.
fair hair
It can also mean 'honest'.
fair play

fare   A noun—what you pay on a train, bus or ferry.
a three dollar **fare**
It can also mean 'food and drink'.
plain **fare**

fate   fete

fate   A noun—the cause of things beyond your control.
It was **fate** that brought us together.

fete   A noun—a fair where people raise money.
The school **fete** was a financial success.

father   farther

father   A noun—a male parent.

farther   An adverb referring to a greater distance.
I ran **farther** than you.

feat   feet

feat   A noun—a deed of great skill, courage or strength.

feet   A noun—you have two of them.

find   fined

find   A verb meaning 'to locate'.
He couldn't **find** his hat.

fined	Past tense of the verb *to fine*—to punish by having to pay money. He was **fined** $100 for a traffic offence.

flour flower

flour	A noun—a powder made from crushed grain. Wholemeal **flour** is good for you.
flower	A noun—the blossom of a plant.
flower	A verb meaning 'to burst into flower'.

for fore four

for	A preposition I sent **for** my servant.
fore	A noun—towards the front. to the **fore**
four	A noun—the number 4.
four	An adjective describing the number of things. **four** calling birds

foul fowl

foul	An adjective meaning 'nasty, dirty, unpleasant'. a **foul** taste
foul	A verb meaning 'to catch or jam'. to **foul** the propeller of a boat
foul	A noun—a breach of a rule in sport. That's a **foul**!
fowl	A noun—a bird, especially a chicken.

grate great

grate	A noun—part of a fireplace or a screen made by a framework of bars. There was a little **grate** near the bottom of the door.
grate	A verb meaning 'to make into smaller portions by rasping or rubbing against a rough surface'. Thomas liked to **grate** carrots. His sister Natalie liked to **grate** cheese.
great	An adjective meaning 'big, large, important'. They had a **great** time at the picnic.

groan grown

groan	A noun—a sound expressing pain or dismay.
groan	A verb meaning 'to make such a sound'.

Homonyms

grown	The past participle of the verb *to grow*.
	I have **grown** two centimetres.
grown	An adjective
	a **grown** man

hall haul

hall	A noun—a corridor, passage or large room.
	assembly **hall**
haul	A noun—an amount taken at one time.
	a **haul** of fish
haul	A verb meaning 'to pull hard'.

heal heel he'll

heal	A verb meaning 'to make well or cure'.
heel	A noun—the back of your foot.
heel	A verb meaning 'follow close at the heels'.
he'll	The contracted form of *he will*.

hear here

hear	A verb
	you **hear** with your ear
here	An adverb of place
	Come **here**!

heard herd

heard	The past tense and past participle of the verb *to hear*.
	I **heard** you.
herd	A noun—a large group of animals.

higher hire

higher	An adjective meaning 'more high'.
	a **higher** jump
higher	An adverb meaning 'more high'.
	He jumped **higher**.
	Both are comparative degree.
hire	A verb meaning 'to pay money to use or employ'.
	to **hire** a boat
hire	A noun
	for **hire**

him hymn

him	A personal pronoun, third person singular number, objective case.
	I saw **him**.

hymn   A noun—a religious song.

hoarse   horse

hoarse   An adjective meaning 'rough or croaky'.
He has a **hoarse** voice.

horse   A noun—a four-legged animal.

hole   whole

hole   A noun—an opening in something.

whole   An adjective meaning 'all of a thing'.
He ate the **whole** cake.

holy   wholly

holy   An adjective meaning 'sacred or religious'.
a **holy** person

wholly   An adverb of degree meaning 'completely'.
He was **wholly** covered by the water.

hour   our

hour   A noun—refers to time.
a full **hour**

our   A possessive adjective
Our book is on the table.

in   inn

in   A preposition
He was **in** the pool.

in   An adverb
Come **in**.

in   An adjective
an **in** group

inn   A noun—a place to stay.
They pulled up at the **inn**.

its   it's

its   A possessive adjective or possessive pronoun
Its feathers were grey.

That is **its** nest.
Its does not have an apostrophe when used this way.

it's   A contraction meaning 'it is'. The apostrophe is needed to show that a letter has been left out.
It's raining today.

key   quay

key   A noun—opens a lock.

quay   A noun—a wharf.

knew new

knew   The past tense of the verb *to know*.

new   An adjective describing something that has just arrived or has just been bought or made.

knight night

knight   A noun—a nobleman who served the king in medieval times; a person who has been knighted and is called Sir; a chess piece.

night   A noun—comes after day.

knot not

knot   A noun—what you tie with string or other material.

knot   A verb meaning 'to tie a knot'.
Knot the rope so it will not slip.

not   A negative adverb
I will **not** do it.

know no

know   A verb meaning 'to understand'.
I **know** where he's hiding.

no   The opposite of yes.
He had **no** shoes to wear.

lead led

lead   A noun (rhymes with *head*)—a heavy, grey metal.
It was as heavy as **lead**.

lead   A verb (rhymes with *feed*) meaning 'to go in front'.
You **lead** and I'll follow.

led   The past tense and past participle of the verb *to lead* (pronounced like *bead*).
He **led** the team onto the field.

loan lone

loan   A noun—something you give for a short time.
I gave him a **loan**.

lone   An adjective describing something by itself.
the **lone** ranger

made maid

made   The past tense or past participle of the verb *to make*.
They **made** a kite.

maid   A noun—an unmarried woman or a female servant.

mail male

mail   A noun—letters sent by post; armour made of metal rings.

mail	A verb meaning 'to send things by post'.
	I will **mail** the letter.
mail	An adjective
	mail delivery
male	A noun—male gender as opposed to female.
male	An adjective
	The **male** lyrebird has a beautiful tail.

main mane

main	An adjective meaning 'the biggest or most important'.
	The **main** road is very long.
main	A noun—the largest pipe in a gas or water system.
mane	A noun—the long hair on the neck of a horse or other animal such as a lion.

mare mayor

mare	A noun—a female horse.
mayor	A noun—the head of a city.

meat meet

meat	A noun—the flesh of an animal.
meet	A verb meaning 'to come face to face with someone'.

medal meddle

medal	A noun—a badge or cross given as a prize or as a reward for bravery.
meddle	A verb meaning 'to interfere'.
	Don't **meddle** in my affairs.

meter metre

meter	A noun—device that measures things that have passed through it.
	water **meter**
	parking **meter**
metre	A noun—a measurement of length.
	This stick is one **metre** long.

miner minor

miner	A noun—one who mines. It is also a type of bird.
minor	An adjective meaning 'smaller in size or importance'.
	The actor had a **minor** part.
minor	A noun—someone who is not an adult.

minute minute

minute	A noun (pronounced *min.et*, with the stress on the first syllable)—a unit of time.

Homonyms

minute An adjective (pronounced *my.nyoot*, with the stress on the last syllable) meaning 'very tiny'.
It was a **minute** creature.

missed mist

missed The past tense or past participle of the verb *to miss*.
I **missed** the bus.
I have **missed** the bus.

mist A noun—like a fog.

morn mourn

morn A noun—a short form of *morning*.

mourn A verb meaning 'to feel sad or show sorrow over someone's death'.

naval navel

naval An adjective meaning 'to do with the navy'.
a **naval** uniform

navel A noun—the small hollow in the middle of your stomach. It is where you were attached to your mother before you were born.

new knew (*see* knew new)

night knight (*see* knight night)

no know (*see* know no)

not knot (*see* knot not)

oar or ore

oar A noun
You row a boat with **oars**.

or A conjunction expressing choice.
oranges **or** lemons

ore A noun—a rock that contains valuable metal.

one won

one A noun—the number 1.

one An adjective
I ate **one** apple.

won The past tense or past participle of the verb *to win*.
I **won** the race.
I have **won** a trip to Tahiti

our hour (*see* hour our)

pain pane

pain A noun—the feeling you have if you hurt yourself.
a **pain** in the neck

pain   A verb meaning 'to cause pain or suffering'.
it **pains** me to tell you

pane   A noun—a sheet of glass in a window.
a window **pane**

pair   pare pear

pair   A noun—two things that go together. Two gloves or shoes form a pair.

pare   A verb meaning 'to cut back or trim away'.

pear   A noun—a fruit.

passed   past

passed   The past tense or past participle of the verb *to pass*.
He **passed** everyone in the race.
I have **passed** my examination.

past   A noun; adjective; adverb; preposition.
a long time ago in the distant **past** [noun]
His **past** achievements are amazing. [adjective]
He went **past**. [adverb]
I walked **past** the window. [preposition]

patience   patients

patience   A noun—what you have when you wait without complaining.

patients   A noun—the plural of *patient*, someone being treated medically.
The doctor's waiting room was full of **patients**.

paw   poor pore pour

paw   A noun—the foot of an animal with nails or claws.

poor   An adjective meaning 'having little money'.
a **poor** person

poor   A noun—poor people as a group.
The **poor** need assistance.

pore   A noun—a tiny opening in the skin.

pore   A verb meaning 'to study something carefully'.
to **pore** over a book

pour   A verb meaning 'to make something flow'.
I will **pour** the milk.

peace   piece

peace   A noun—no war; quietness.
'Give me a bit of **peace**,' Mum said.

piece   A noun—a part.
: a **piece** of pie
  It can also mean 'a single thing'.
  a **piece** of fruit

piece   A verb meaning 'to fit together'.
: to **piece** a jigsaw together

plain   plane

plain   A noun—a large, flat area of land.
: a grassy **plain**

plain   An adjective meaning 'clear and simple; not beautiful'.
: a **plain** statement
: a **plain** face

plane   A noun—the abbreviated form of *aeroplane*.
: the **plane** to Melbourne
  Also a tool used in woodworking.
  a smoothing **plane**

plane   A verb meaning 'to make smooth'.
: He **planed** the timber.

practice   practise

practice   A noun (the 'c' in *practice* always tells you it is a noun)—a thing you do over and over, or the usual way of doing something.
: I went to football **practice**.
: It is the best **practice**.

practise   A verb (the 's' in *practise* always tells you that it is a verb) meaning 'to do something over and over'.
: I will **practise** my tennis.

principal   principle

principal   A noun—the head of a school or other institution.

principal   An adjective meaning 'the main person or thing'.
: the **principal** actor on the stage

principle   A noun—a rule or something you believe is right.
: He had the highest **principles**.

quay   key (see key quay)

rain   reign   rein

rain   A noun—water from the sky.

rain   A verb meaning 'to fall from the sky in drops'.
: It **rained** all day.

reign   A verb meaning 'to rule like a king or queen'.

rein   A noun—a leather strap used to guide or drive a horse.
He held the **reins** in his hand.

rap   wrap

rap   A noun—a sharp, short knock.

rap   A verb meaning 'to make a sharp, short knock'.
to **rap** on the door

rap   An adjective describing a form of dancing and music.
rap dancing

wrap   A verb meaning 'to cover'.
I will **wrap** the present.

wrap   A noun—a covering.

raw   roar

raw   An adjective meaning 'not cooked' or 'not trained'.
raw meat
raw recruit

roar   A noun—a loud, deep sound.
a lion's **roar**

roar   A verb meaning 'to make a loud, deep sound'.
The lion **roared**.

read   red

read   The past tense and past participle of the verb *to read*.
I **read** the book yesterday.

red   A noun—the name of the colour.

red   An adjective
The girl had **red** hair.

read   reed

read   A verb—to get meaning from the printed word.
He could **read** at six.

reed   A noun—an aquatic plant.
He pulled a **reed** out of the creek.

real   reel

real   An adjective meaning 'the genuine thing'.
a **real** life story

reel   A noun—something you wind things onto; a Scottish dance.

reel   A verb meaning 'to wind in'; 'to stagger or sway'.

right   rite   write

right   An adjective meaning 'correct' or 'not left'.
You are **right**. Good work!

Correct usage

right	An adverb
	Turn **right** at the next corner.
right	A noun—a fair claim.
	You have a **right** to enter.
rite	A noun—a ceremony, usually religious.
write	A verb meaning 'to make letters or words with a pen, pencil or other device'.

ring wring

ring	A noun—a circular band such as a wedding ring, or anything shaped like a ring.
	a key **ring**, a circus **ring**, a boxing **ring**
wring	A verb meaning 'to squeeze'.
	I'll **wring** your neck if you don't behave!

road rode rowed

road	A noun—a track for people to travel along.
rode	The past tense of the verb *to ride*.
	I **rode** the horse yesterday.
rowed	The past tense of the verb *to row*.
	We **rowed** in the regatta.

root route

root	A noun—the part of a plant that grows in the soil.
route	A noun—the way you take to go from one place to another.
	This is the bus **route**.

row row

row	A noun (rhymes with *so*)—a line of things.
	a **row** of birds on the fence
row	A verb (rhymes with *so*)
	to **row** a boat
row	A noun (rhymes with *cow*)—a noisy quarrel.

sail sale

sail	A noun
	the **sail** of a boat
sail	A verb meaning 'to move over water, usually in a craft'.
	I **sail** every Saturday.
sale	A noun—where you go to buy things cheaply.
sale	An adjective
	sale price

sauce source

sauce   A noun—what you pour on a pie.

source   A noun—the place where something starts.
The **source** of the river is in the mountains.

saw soar sore

saw   A noun—a tool with sharp teeth.

saw   A verb describing what you do with a saw.
I will **saw** the wood.

saw   The past tense of the verb *to see*.
I **saw** the movie.

soar   A verb meaning 'to fly upward or float in the sky'.
to **soar** like an eagle

sore   An adjective meaning 'painful'.
She has a **sore** foot.

sore   A noun
a **sore** on your leg

scene seen

scene   A noun—the place in which the action of a play takes place; a portion of a play.
The **scene** was a darkened dungeon.

seen   Past tense of the verb *to see*.
Have you **seen** the way I dance?

sea see

sea   A noun—a large stretch of water.

see   A verb describing what your eyes do.

seam seem

seam   A noun—where two pieces of cloth are joined.

seem   A verb meaning 'to appear to be'.
They **seem** happy.

seas sees seize

seas   A noun—the plural of *sea*.

sees   A verb—part of the verb *to see*.
He **sees** the train coming.

seize   A verb meaning 'to grab hold of something suddenly'.
Seize him!

sell cell (*see* cell sell)

sent cent scent (*see* cent sent scent)

serial cereal (*see* cereal serial)

sew so sow

- sew A verb meaning 'to join with stitches'.
- so An adverb that has many meanings. Here are some:
  Do not walk **so** fast.
  Is that **so**?
  You are **so** kind.
- sow A verb meaning 'to spread seeds on the earth'.
- sow A noun (rhymes with *cow*)—a female pig.

shear sheer

- shear A verb meaning 'to cut the hair or wool from an animal'.
  It is time to **shear** the sheep.
  The plural, *shears*, is a noun meaning 'the large clippers used to cut the wool'.
- sheer An adjective meaning 'very thin, so that you can see through'.
  sheer curtains
  It also means 'complete or absolute'.
  sheer luck
  It can mean 'very steep' as well.
  a **sheer** drop

side sighed

- side A noun—the edges of an object; a position.
  She touched the **side** of the car.
- sighed Past tense of the verb *to sigh*.
  He **sighed**, he cried and nearly died.

sight site cite (*see* cite sight site)

some sum

- some An adjective that does not tell exactly how many or how much.
  There are **some** apples in the basket.
  There is **some** mud on your shoes.
- sum A noun—a total.
  the **sum** of all these numbers

son sun

- son A noun—the male child of someone.
- sun A noun—the bright star that warms the Earth and lights the sky.

stair stare

stair — A noun—one of a number of steps.

stare — A verb meaning 'to look at someone or something for a long time'.

stake steak

stake — A noun—a stick you can push into the ground.

steak — A noun—a thick piece of meat or fish for grilling or frying.

stalk stork

stalk — A noun—the stem of a plant.

stalk — A verb meaning 'to follow something very quietly'.
The lion **stalks** its prey.

stork — A noun—a bird with long legs.

stationary stationery

stationary — An adjective describing something that is still.
The stork was **stationary**.

stationery — A noun—writing paper and other writing material.
The stationer sells **stationery**.

steal steel

steal — A verb meaning 'to take something that does not belong to you'.

steel — A noun—a tough material made from iron and other things.

steel — An adjective
a **steel** helmet

steel — A verb meaning 'to harden'.
Steel yourself; they're attacking.

storey story

storey — A noun—one whole level of a building.

story — A noun—a tale.
He told us an exciting **story**.

straight strait

straight — An adjective meaning 'not bent or crooked'; 'honest' or 'serious'.

strait — A noun—a narrow channel joining two bodies of water.
Bass **Strait**

tail tale

tail — A noun
A dog has a **tail**.

tale — A noun—a story.

tear tear

tear — A noun (rhymes with *dear*)—what rolls from your eyes when you cry.

tear — A noun (rhymes with *bear*)—a rip in something.
a **tear** in his pants

tear — A verb (rhymes with *bear*) meaning 'to rip something'.
She could **tear** her dress if she climbed that fence.

their there they're

their — A possessive adjective used to show that something belongs to more than one person.
Their noses are cold.

there — An adverb meaning 'in that place'.
It is over **there**.

they're — The contraction of *they are*.
They're coming to see us.

theirs there's

theirs — A possessive pronoun.
Our project is great. **Theirs** is rubbish.

there's — The contraction of *there is*.
There's a cow in the front garden.

threw through

threw — The past tense of the verb *to throw*.
Jenny **threw** the ball further than I.

through — Often a preposition beginning a phrase.
The ship passed **through** the canal.

tied tide

tied — The past tense and past participle of the verb *to tie*.
I **tied** the horse to the gate.
I have **tied** my shoelace with a double knot.

tide — A noun—the rise and fall of the ocean.

to too two

to — A preposition meaning 'towards'.
Come **to** me.
They ran **to** the fence.
to is also part of the infinitive of verbs.
to eat, **to** sleep.

too — An adverb meaning 'also'.
He came, **too**.
It can also mean 'more than what is wanted'.
too fat

two	A noun—the number 2.
two	An adjective **two** brown cows

toe tow

toe	A noun. You have five **toes** at the end of each foot.
tow	A verb. You tow something if you drag it along using a rope or chain.

wail whale

wail	A verb meaning 'to make a long, mournful cry'.
whale	A noun—a large mammal that lives in the sea.

waist waste

waist	A noun—the middle part of your body, just above your hips.
waste	A verb meaning 'to use something in an extravagant way'. Don't **waste** water!
waste	A noun They collected their **waste**.
waste	An adjective He is a **waste** collector.

wait weight

wait	A verb meaning 'to stay somewhere'. **Wait** at the bus stop.
weight	A noun—a measure of heaviness. What is the **weight** of this bag?

ware wear where

ware	A noun—goods that a merchant sells. It is often plural and often joined to other words, for example *hardware*. Dad bought a new trowel at the hard**ware** shop.
wear	A verb meaning 'to be dressed in something'. Did you **wear** your new suit?
where	An adverb or conjunction asking 'in what place'. **Where** did you get that funny hat?

way weigh

way	A noun—how to do something; the path you take. That is the right **way**. This is the **way** to the airport.
weigh	A verb meaning 'to find out how heavy a thing is'. **Weigh** yourself on the scales.

weak week

weak An adjective meaning 'not strong or powerful'.
He is a very **weak** person.
I like **weak** tea.

week A noun—a period of seven days.

weather wether whether

weather A noun—sunshine, rain, cloud, wind or snow.

wether A noun—a ram that cannot breed.

whether A conjunction meaning 'if it is the case that'.
I asked **whether** he was going.

we'd weed

we'd Contraction of 'we would'.
We'd better behave on the excursion.

weed A noun—a nuisance plant.
A **weed** came up in the middle of his potato patch.

weed A verb—the act of removing weeds from the garden.
I often help Dad **weed** the herb garden.

which witch

which A relative pronoun
Which would you like?
We ate apples **which** were delicious.

witch A noun—a woman who carries out magic.

whole hole (*see* hole whole)

wholly holy (*see* holy wholly)

who's whose

who's The contraction of *who is*.

whose A possessive pronoun or possessive adjective showing ownership.

wind wind

wind A noun (rhymes with *thinned*)—moving air.

wind A verb (rhymes with *bind*) meaning 'to change direction or twist around'.
The road seemed to **wind** round the mountain.
Wind the clock.

won one (*see* one won)

wood would

wood A noun—the hard part of a tree. Also means 'land covered by trees'.
I walked through the **wood**.

would	A verb	
	I **would** like an apple.	

wound wound

wound	A noun (rhymes with *tuned*)—an injury.
wound	(rhymes with *hound*) The past tense and past participle of the verb *to wind*.
	He **wound** the fishing line onto the cork.

wrap **rap** (*see* rap wrap)

wring **ring** (*see* ring wring)

write **right rite** (*see* right rite write)

yew **ewe you** (*see* ewe yew you)

yore **your you're**

yore	A noun—old times; a long time ago.
	in days of **yore**
your	A possessive adjective
	Your homework was very untidy.
you're	The contracted form of *you are*.
	Are you sure **you're** coming to my birthday party?

Making sense

🍎 Errors to avoid

Absolute words

Some words are complete in themselves; they cannot be more or less.

✅ Everything is *perfect*.

Not

❌ Everything is ~~more perfect~~.

Other absolute words are:

| alive | correct | dead | final | unique |

Agreement

Words in sentences must agree in person and number.

✅ The captain of the team will make *his* (or *her*) decision.

Not

❌ The captain of the team will make ~~their~~ decision.

✅ Each child in the class *is* writing.

Not

❌ Each child in the class ~~are~~ writing.

Dangling words and phrases (dangling modifiers)

Do not leave words or phrases dangling. That is, they must be correctly attached to their nouns, pronouns or verbs.

✅ While I was answering the telephone, the cat ate the fish

Not

❌ ~~While answering the telephone the cat ate the fish~~.

(See **Words in the wrong place** p. 146)

Double negatives

Do not use double negatives.

If you write ***I don't know nothing***, it means that you must know something. That is not usually what you mean.

Matching lists or series

Make sure that lists or series match.

✅ You can go by train, bus, car or plane.
Not
❌ ~~You can go by train, bus, car or fly.~~

(unless you mean this)

going by fly

🍎 Improving your writing

Clichés

Clichés (pronounced **klee-shays**) are tired old words and phrases. Avoid them.

Some clichés are:
  old as the hills
  fat as a pig
  sick as a dog
  thin as a rake

sick as a dog

Clichés **can** be used in conversation to give special effects. Always try to find fresh, new comparisons if you can.

Double meanings

Dangling modifiers cause double meanings. Watch out for double meanings at all times.

  eating apples

might mean apples that are good for eating, that someone is eating apples, or that the apples are eating.

  beautiful girl's dress

might mean the dress of a beautiful girl or the beautiful dress of a girl.

*(See **Words with different meanings** p. 146)*

Mixed ideas (mixed metaphors)

Mixed metaphors are like mixed lists.

Do not mix ideas in sentences.

Do not write:

  They flew at each other like raging elephants.

(Elephants are not likely to fly).

Overused words

Try to find other words for **nice**, **fantastic**, **brilliant** and **great**. They are overused.

It is better to write

    He is a very friendly (or pleasant) person.

than

    He is a very nice person.

It is better to write

    The movie was interesting (or fascinating).

than

    The movie was fantastic.

Other overused words are:

    awesome   fabulous   got   tremendous

You can leave out *got* on many occasions.

It is better to write

    I have a red bike.

than

    I have got a red bike.

Prepositions at the ends of sentences

Try not to use prepositions at the ends of sentences.

It is better to write

    I fell into this water.

than

    This is the water I fell into.

Sexist language

If you use words in ways that leave out males or females when they should be included, you are using sexist language.

It is better to write

    firefighter   doctor   actor   nurse

than

    fireman/firewoman   lady doctor   actress   male nurse.

Slang

Slang is everyday, informal, spoken language that is not used in writing, except for special effects.

It is better to write

    I feel sick.

than

> I feel crook.

It is better to write

> Throw me the ball.

than

> Chuck me the ball.

Split infinitive

It is better in most cases to keep both parts of the infinitive together.

It is better to write

> to walk quickly

than

> to quickly walk.

Unnecessary words

Do not use words that mean the same as others.

It is better to write

> I believe what you say.

than

> I, personally, believe what you say.

It is better to write

> advance   descend   my autobiography

than

> advance forward   descend downwards   my own autobiography.

Vague words

Do not use vague words when you need to be precise.

> a big man

may be tall or fat or both.

Say exactly what you mean.

a big man   **a big man**   **a big man**

Wordiness (too many words)

Some people use too many words to say something.

The rule is: **be economical**.

It is better to write.

    now

than

    at this point in time.

Words in the wrong place

Be careful where you place words, like adverbs, in sentences.

This sentence does not have a precise meaning because of the place of the word **only**.

    Tennis shoes only will be worn on the court.

Note: In this case it would be better to rewrite the sentence with something like this:

    Tennis shoes will be the only footwear permitted on this court.

OR Players must wear tennis shoes.

Words with different meanings

If words have different meanings, use them with care.

    'Throw down your arms!' shouted the general.

Origins of words and figurative language

Origins of words

Modern English has borrowed from the languages of many countries in the world and is still doing so. Knowing the origins of words and their parts helps us read, write and understand our language better. Here are some examples of word origins:

navy	from the Latin word **navis**, a ship
history	from the Greek word meaning **knowledge**
poultry	from the French word **poule**, a hen
halt	from the German word **halten**, to stop
kimono	from the Japanese word meaning **a loose robe**
submarine	from the Latin prefix **sub**, meaning **under**, and the Latin root or base word **mare** meaning **the sea**

School dictionaries often do not tell you the origins of words. You may need to look in a larger dictionary.

🍎 Figurative language

There are many devices in English that make our language colourful. They help to make our writing rich and varied. Here are some of them:

Alliteration: the repetition of the first sounds in words.

    ruby red rose

Idiom: the everyday use of colourful expressions special to a particular country or its language.

    dob in (to tell on someone)

    pull your head in (shut up)

Metaphor: a direct comparison.

    The moon was a ghostly galleon.

Onomatopoeia: a device in which the sense is suggested by the sound of the word.

    the wind whistled

    a rustle in the leaves

    the screech of brakes

Personification: a device that gives lifeless things the qualities of a living creature.

    The trees bowed in the wind.

    The flames licked at the walls of the house.

Simile: the comparison of two things with *like* or *as*.

    as pretty as a picture

    He was like a lion in battle.

Index

abbreviations	91–2
absolute words	18, 142
abstract nouns	1, 2
acronyms	91–2
adjectival clauses	45, 51
adjectival (or adjective) phrases	39–40, 83, 85
adjectivals	81, 87
adjective group	83
adjectives	
-ly	31
and commas	93
definition	15, 80
degrees of comparison	17
demonstrative	9, 16
descriptive or describing	15
classifying	15
compound	98
factual	15
distinctive	10
distributive	10, 16
fewer and *less*	18
indefinite	17
infinitives that act as adjectives	29
interrogative	8, 16
job	42
modal	17
numeral or numbering	16, 98
positive only	18
possessive	7, 15
that are participles	6
verbal *see* participles, present	
adverb group	80, 83
adverbial clauses	44–5, 51, 81, 88
adverbial (or adverb) phrases	40, 41, 83, 85
adverbials	81, 87–8
adverbs	
-ly	31
and commas	93
definition	29
degrees of comparison	31–2
infinitives that act as adverbs	29
job	42
for text cohesion	83
types	30
adverbs of degree	31
interrogative	30
manner	30
modal	31, 82
negative	30
numerical	31
place	30
reason	30
time	30, 82
use	30
alliteration	147
antecedent	7, 8, 11, 12, 45
antonyms	54
apostrophes	95–6
articles, definite and indefinite	36
attribute	80, 81, 85
auxiliary verbs	19, 21, 26–7, 82, 85
to be	
chart of tense forms	26
and the nominative case	14
noun clause after part of verb *to be*	46
as part of an adjectival phrase	40
as a relating or linking verb	19
use with other verbs	21, 23, 26
brackets	97

capital letters	90, 98
causality	88
circumstances	80, 81, 85, 86, 88
clause complex	86, 88
clauses	
adjectival	45, 51
adverbial	44–5, 51, 81
and commas	93–4
definition	43, 85
embedded	87, 88
and finite verb	20
noun	45–6, 51
principal or independent	43, 44, 48–9, 51, 86, 87, 93
restrictive and non-restrictive	89
subordinate or dependent	43, 44, 48–9, 87
clichés	143
closed words	89
coda	58
cohesion	54, 80, 82–3, 85
collective nouns	1, 2
collocation	55, 88
colons	97
commands	47, 49–50, 80, 81, 86
commas	
with adjectives and adverbs	93
with compound sentences	93
with direct speech	94
and lists	92–3
use and meaning	50, 92, 96–7
with words, phrases and clauses	
beginning a sentence	93
within a sentence	93–4
common gender nouns	5, 12–13
common nouns	1
complement	14, 46, 104
concrete nouns	3
confused words, correct usage of	99–141
conjunctions	
and connectives	55
coordinate	34, 48, 93
correlative	34–5
definition	34, 80, 85
subordinate	35, 45, 48–9
for text cohesion	83
that exist in pairs	34–5
connectives	55, 93, 96
content words	89
contractions	95, 96
could	19
count and mass nouns	2–3
cultural context	79
dangling modifiers	142, 143
dashes	97–8
declarative mood	80, 81, 86
degree	
adverbs of	31
of comparison	17, 31–2
of usuality, certainty or obligation	82
description, factual	62, 67
description, literary	61–4
determiners	88
dialogue patterns	56
different from	33, 105
direct speech	90, 94–5
discussion	75–7
double meanings	143
double negative	142
each	10, 16, 102

Index

either	10, 16, 105	hyphens	98
ellipsis	83, 85, 98	*I*	6, 24–5, 90
empty	18	idiom	147
every	16	imperative mood	25, 80, 81, 86
exclamation marks	92, 94	indicative mood	25, 81, 86
exclamations	47, 50, 94	indirect object	6–7
explanation	72–3	indirect speech	90–1, 95
exposition	54, 73–5	infinitive phrases	42
feminine nouns	5, 12	infinitives	
few	17	and adjectival phrases	40
fewer	18	and adverbial phrases	40, 41
field (of a text)	79, 80	definition	20–1
figurative language	147	as nouns, adjectives or adverbs	29
full	18	and present participles	21
full stops	90–2, 94, 96	split	145
see also ellipsis		inflection	86
functional grammar	vi, 52, 85–7	information report	68–9
future continuous tense	24	interjections	37
future perfect continuous tense	24	interrogative mood	80, 81, 86
future perfect tense	24	*it*	6, 7, 25
future tense	23, 87	*its*	7, 15, 96, 128
genres see text types (genres)		*it's*	96, 128
gerund phrases	42	language, spoken and written	57, 77–8, 144–5
gerunds	5–6, 29, 41	*less*	18
got	144	lexical cohesion (related words)	83, 85
grammatical words	89	lists	92–3, 96, 97, 142–3
to *have*	19, 24, 109	*many*	17, 111
he	6, 25, 109	masculine nouns	5, 12
head word	88	*may*	19, 103
her	7, 15	*me*	6, 7, 111
hers	7, 96	meanings, different	146
him	7, 109, 127	metalanguage	vi
his	7, 15, 96	metaphors	147
homographs	56	mixed	143
homonyms	56, 117–41		
homophones	56		

150

might	19
mine	7
modal group	80
modality	80, 82, 86, 88
mode (of a text)	79, 80
modifiers	86, 87, 88, 142, 143
mood	25, 80, 81, 86
morphemes, free and bound	88–9
morphology	88–9
most	17
must	19, 80, 82
my	6, 15, 111
narrative	52, 54, 58–61
neither	10, 16, 105
neuter nouns	5, 12
nominal group	80, 83
nominalisation	80, 89
nominative case	
finding	5
personal pronouns	6, 13, 14
and the verb *to be*	14
and *who*	7
noun group	80, 81, 83, 84, 86
noun phrase	41, 81, 83
nouns	
case	5
compound	4, 98
definition	1, 86
gender	5, 12
infinitives that act as nouns	29
job	42
making plurals	3–4, 96
number	3–4, 7
as participants	80, 81, 84
person	3, 7
and prepositions	33
and relative pronouns	7
singular	3–4
types	1–3, 90
use in text cohesion	82
verbal *see* gerunds	
numbers	16, 96, 98
object	
noun clause as	45–6
noun phrase as	41
personal pronoun as	6–7
of a verb, finding	22
objective case	
finding	5
personal pronouns	7, 13
and *whom*	8
onomatopoeia	147
onto	33
open words	89
origins of words	146–7
our	7, 15, 128
ours	7, 96
overused words	143–4
paragraphs	52–3
parentheses	97
parsing	38
participants	80, 81, 84, 86
participial phrases	42
participles	
definition	86
past *(-ed)*	21, 23, 27, 28, 39
present *(-ing)*	6, 18, 21, 23, 28, 39
past continuous tense	24
past perfect continuous tense	24
past perfect tense	24
past tense	23, 28, 87

Index

personification	147	continuous tense	24
phrases		present perfect tense	24
adjectival (or adjective)	39–40, 83, 85	present tense	23, 87
		timeless	23, 84, 87, 89
adverbial (or adverb)	83, 85	procedural recount	69
of manner	40	procedure	52, 54, 69, 70
of place	40	processes	80, 81, 84, 86, 87
of reason	41	pronominal (or pronoun)	
of time	40	adjectives	7, 8, 9, 10, 15
and commas	93–4	pronouns	
definition	39, 86	case	5, 13
noun	41, 81, 83	definition	6, 80, 81, 86
prepositional	41–2, 80, 86	demonstrative	8
verbal or verb	41–2, 81, 83	distributive	10
placement of words	146	emphatic *(-self, -selves)*	9
poetry	57, 66–7, 97	gender	12–13
possessive case		indefinite *(-one, -body, -thing)*	9, 100–1, 106
finding	5	interrogative	8
personal pronouns	13	number	11–12
predicate	47, 86	person	3, 7
prefixes	98	*first*	10, 22
prepositional phrases	41–2, 80, 86	*second*	10–11, 22
prepositions		*third*	11, 22
and adjectival phrases	39	personal	6–7, 13, 14
and adverbial phrases	40	possessive	7, 96
common	32	and prepositions	7, 13, 33
definition	32, 86	reflexive *(-self, -selves)*	9
at the end of a sentence	144	relative	7–8, 45, 48
finding	33	for text cohesion	82
and noun clauses	46	and use of apostrophe	96
and the objective case	5	and the verb *to be*	14
and pronouns	7, 13, 33	proper nouns	1, 90
special	33	punctuation	50, 90–8
and *whom*	8	quantity adjectives	16, 98
present continuous tense	24	question marks	92, 94
present perfect			

question pronouns	8
questions	47, 50, 80, 81, 86, 89, 92, 94
quotation marks	90, 94–5
quotations	95, 97
recount, factual	54, 61, 70–1
recount, literary	60–1
reference	82, 85
register	56, 77, 79
related words (lexical cohesion)	83, 85
relating verbs	19
repetition	54
review, literary	64–6
rheme	54, 80, 82, 86
to seem	19, 46, 137
semicolons	96–7
sentences	
analysis	51
complex	47, 48–9
compound (combined)	47, 48
definition and types	47, 80, 81, 86
and finite verb	20, 51
punctuation	50, 90–8
simple	47–8
that are both compound and complex	49
that end with a preposition	144
topic	53
sexist language	144
shall	24–5, 114
she	6
should	80, 82
simile	147
slang	144–5
social context	77, 79
some	17, 136
split infinitive	145
statements	47, 50, 80, 81, 86, 94
structures	
clause	81
language	81–3
text	52
word	80
subject	
in active and passive voice	87
definition	86
of a finite verb, finding	20
and finite verbs in sentences	47–9
noun clause as	45–6
noun phrase as	41
understood	49–50
subjective case *see* nominative case	
subjunctive mood	25, 86
substitution	82, 85
synonyms	54
tag questions	89
technical nouns	2
tenor (of a text)	79, 80
tense	
continuous form	23
definition	87
past tense and past participle	28
perfect continuous form	23, 24
perfect form	24
simple form	23
timeless present tense	23, 84, 87, 89
terms of address nouns	2
text links	54
text types (genres)	
factual	52, 57, 67–77
literary	52, 57, 58–67

overview	52, 57, 79	irregular	21, 27–8
texts, differences in	52–4, 79	*common*	28
that	7, 8, 16, 45, 46, 115	linking	19
their	7, 15, 115, 138	modal	19
theirs	7, 96, 115, 138	mood	25, 80, 81, 86
them	6, 7, 115–16	negative forms	20, 142
theme (of a clause)	54, 80, 82, 86, 87	non-finite	20
these	8, 16, 115	participles *see* participles	
they	6, 25, 115–16	as processes	80, 81, 84, 86, 87
this	8, 16, 115	singular	11, 22–3
those	8, 16, 115, 116	strong *see* verbs, irregular	
titles	90, 95	tense *see* tense	
to appear	46	transitive	22
to become	46	types	19
to look	46	voice	25–6, 80, 87
to remain	46	weak	28
topic sentence	53	voice, active and	
traditional grammar	vi, 52, 85–7	passive	25–6, 80, 87
unnecessary words	145	*we*	6, 24
us	7	*what*	8, 16, 116
vague words	145	*where*	45
verb group	80, 81, 83, 87	*which*	7, 8, 16, 45, 116, 140
verbal (or verb) phrases	41–2, 81, 83	*who*	7–8, 45
verbs		*whom*	7–8, 45
agreement with subject	22–3, 142	*whose*	8, 16, 140
auxiliary (helping)	20, 21, 27, 82, 85	*will*	19, 24–5, 82, 114
chart of regular verbs	27	word chains	55
compound	27	word families	55
definition	19, 81, 84, 87	word sets or clusters	55
finite	20, 43, 47–9, 50, 51, 85, 86	wordiness	146
infinitives *see* infinitives		*you*	6, 7, 25, 125
intransitive	22	*your*	7, 15, 141
		yours	7, 96